NOTICING
NEWTON ABBOT

AN EXPLORATION OF THE TOWN'S BUILDINGS, PEOPLE AND EVENTS

Illustrated with drawings by Ewan Walton,
photographs and words by Tess Walker

A catalogue record for this book is available from the British Library.

ISBN 978-0-9933352-5-9

Published by We Make Magazines Ltd on behalf of Tess Walker
wemakemagazines.co.uk

Thanks to Michael Bennie for copy editing and proof-reading and to Katy Bennie for overall organisation of the team.

Thanks to Historic England's Heritage Schools Programme for funding the creation of new artistic work by Ewan Walton.

Thanks to Newton Abbot Town Museum for free access to their archives and for putting in the first order for copies of this book.

wemakemagazines

Introduction

The descriptions of the listed buildings have been compiled by English Heritage, now Historic England, since 1949. The work of the surveyors has been immense and without their scrutiny of the buildings and structures of our country, which many people ignore and some think unworthy, our heritage would be diminished. They and our elected councillors follow the wise legislation put in place to protect these buildings after the Second World War, but the owner of the building must be thanked – or reviled – for the way in which they have maintained the building they hold in trust for future generations.

The Buildings

In the Second World War, many buildings in the UK were damaged by bombs and fires. In the urgency to reconstruct our cities many buildings were demolished, but some of these could have been repaired. It was this awareness which prompted the passing of the Town and Country Planning Act in 1947, one element of which was to create a Statutory List of buildings and structures of Special Architectural or Historic Interest. Buildings on this list are protected from alteration, both inside and outside, and from demolition unless consent is given by the local Planning Authority (locally Teignbridge District Council).

Listed buildings are classified into three grades:

- Grade I: of exceptional interest, sometimes considered to be internationally important.
- Grade II*: particularly important buildings.
- Grade II: locally important and of special interest.

There are about 500,000 listed buildings in the UK. Newton Abbot and immediate area has over 160 including four at grade I; five at grade II*. Many of these were added to the Statutory List in the first survey of 1949, and the remainder in later revisions or if the building was put at risk by redevelopment.

Buildings are most common on the List, but Newton Abbot also has listed bridges, gravestones, war memorials, milestones, walls, railings and gateposts.

The written description of a listed building uses specialist architectural terms – shorthand for those who speak the same language, but impenetrable to most.

This book tries to describe the more interesting buildings in Newton Abbot using a simpler language, photographs by Tess Walker and drawings by Ewan Walton.

Piecemeal damage has been done to many buildings by wiring, alarm systems, ventilation, shop signs, satellite dishes and aerials which have been added and abandoned. Some of the photographs in the book have been 'cleaned' so that the glory of the building can be shown without these distractions.

The Interesting People and Events

The Newton Abbot we know today was once two settlements on either side of the River Lemon: Newton Abbot (Wolborough) and Newton Bushel (Highweek). They became one town in 1901.

Thousands of people have lived and worked in Wolborough and Highweek parishes. Their lives were ordinary and extraordinary. Some of their stories are also related here as they bring the history alive.

References

- British Newspaper Archive
- Public records accessed through Ancestry.com
- Historic England's Statutory List
- *Pevsner's Architectural Glossary.* Yale University Press and Aimer Media, 2016. Version 1.1. Apple App Store

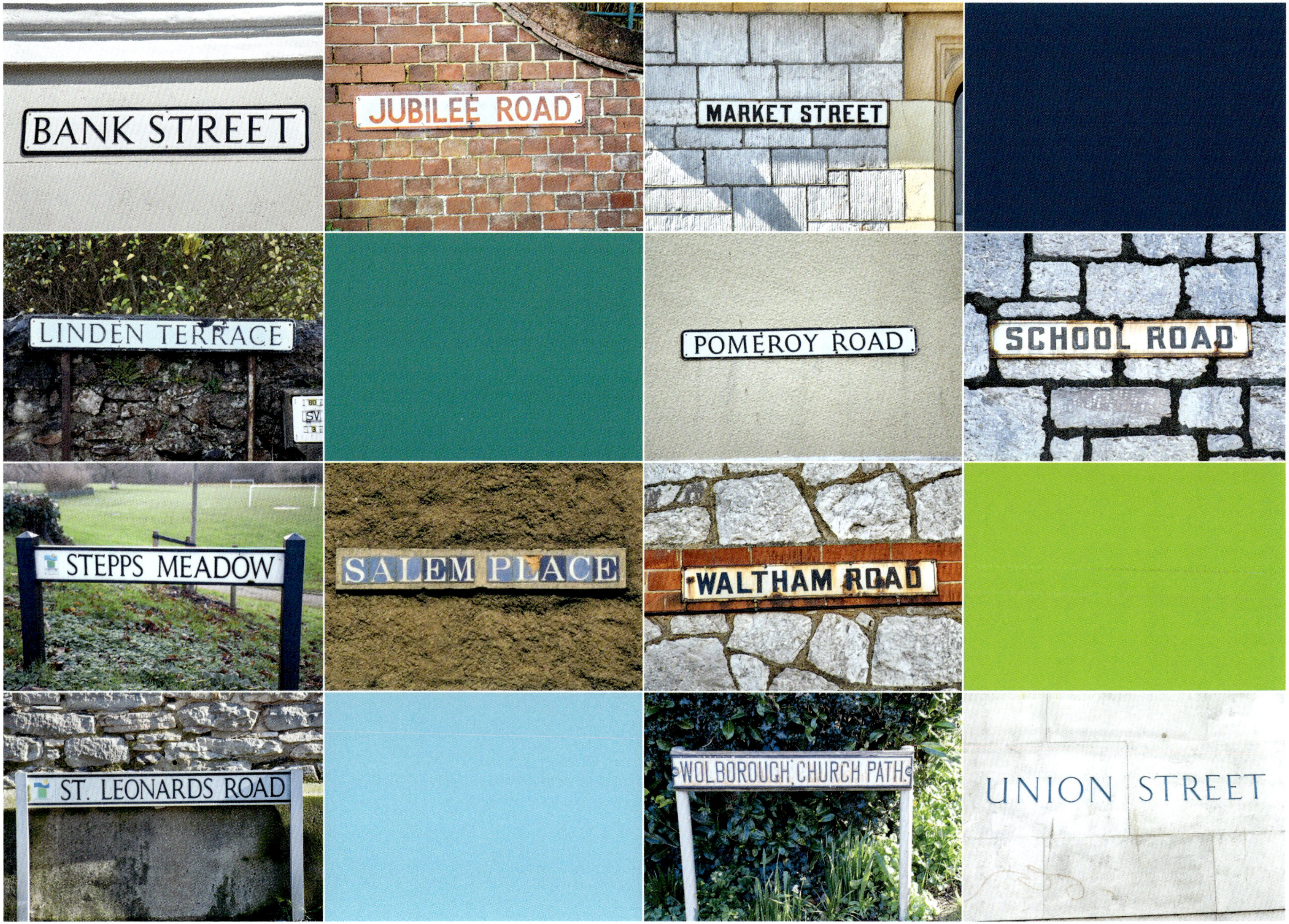
BANK STREET
JUBILEE ROAD
MARKET STREET
LINDEN TERRACE
POMEROY ROAD
SCHOOL ROAD
STEPPS MEADOW
SALEM PLACE
WALTHAM ROAD
ST. LEONARDS ROAD
WOLBOROUGH CHURCH PATH
UNION STREET

Contents

Newton Abbot:

Through the eyes of an artist

I know my town really well. Of course I do, I've lived here for ages. At least that's what I thought before joining Tess Walker to produce this book. 'The devil is in the detail' as the saying goes, and it would appear that Newton Abbot is a case in point. Whilst it was an education in itself for me to become better acquainted with some of the town's grander buildings, like the examples I have drawn in colour, Tess's research has uncovered a wealth of historical interest and a fascinating cast of characters behind many of the smaller, more easily missed features of Newton Abbot. So, what does this have to do with drawing? Well, the eyes of the artist now see differently, viewing every doorway, wall and window with a degree of suspicion... Just what did happen here?

Ewan Walton

St. Leonard's Chapel Tower

Wolborough Street. Page 78

I had drawn St. Leonard's Chapel Tower in black and white as a commission some years ago, so I knew what the challenges were. The perspective points on either side have been brought in closer to the edges of the drawing, which although easier to work with, does produce a more dramatic view. In this drawing you can see much more of the surrounding buildings, which all give clues of their own as to when in history the scene is set. The colours I have chosen are really on an aesthetic basis and have all been correct at some point, but not necessarily at the same time.

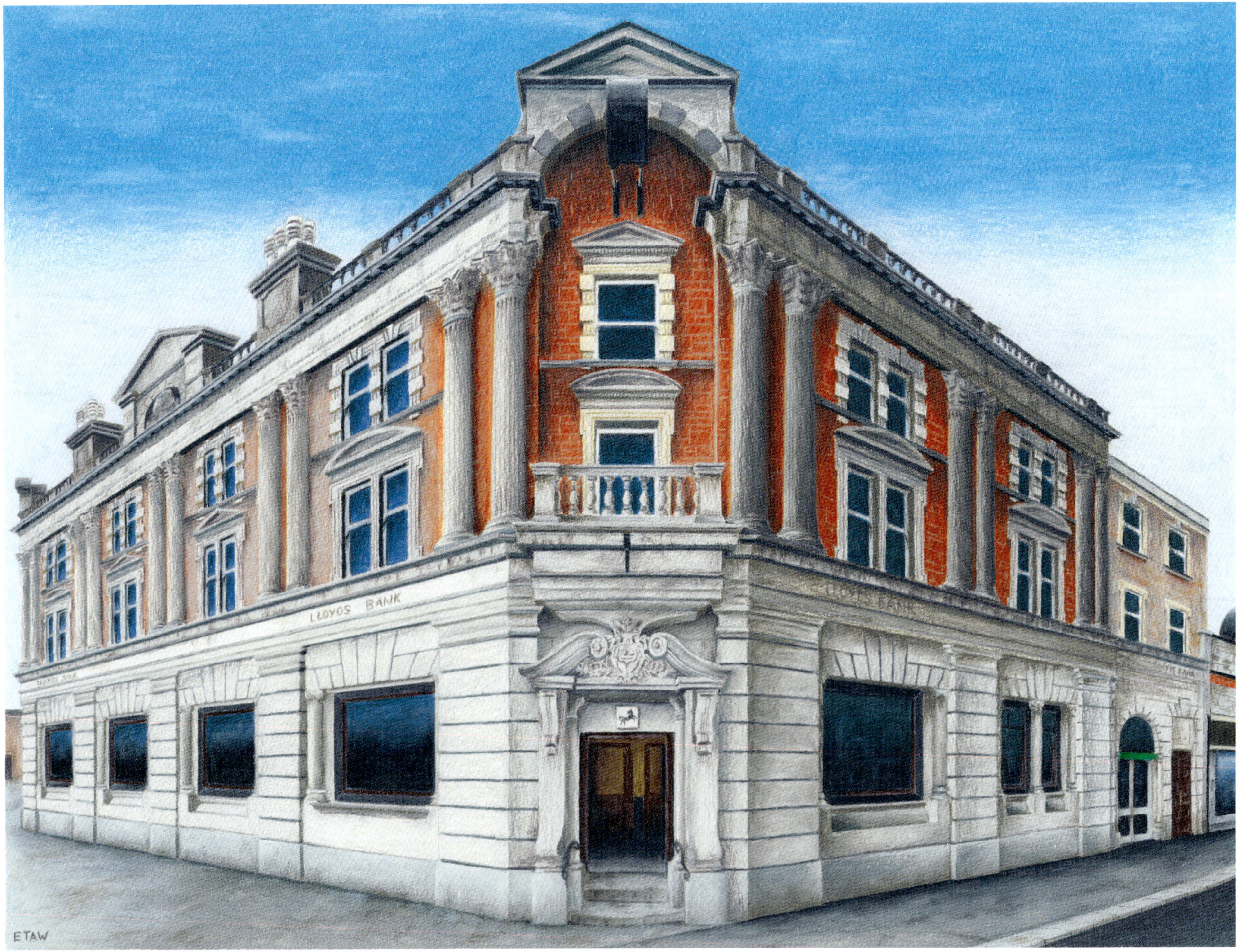
LLOYDS BANK
ETAW

Lloyds Bank

Courtenay Street. Page 32

"For some reason or other, this is the drawing I struggled with the most. There's a lot of complexity in the top half of the building and the Corinthian pillars are tricky. The coloured pencils I used for this piece are rich and waxy, but on reflection I think a harder pencil would have enabled a more successful rendering. That said, there is much to be happy about; the detail above the entrance and the definition of the stonework on the lower half of the building have come out very well."

ETAW

Bradley Manor

Totnes Road. Page 111

I'm really pleased with this one; I think the setting in amongst the trees makes for a satisfying composition, as well as providing a bit more variety when it comes to drawing. At first glance I thought this would be fairly straightforward, but then, as I looked a bit more closely, the symmetry vanished. Nothing here is symmetrical. The windows do not sit centrally within their section of the building façade, they are at differing heights and are of differing designs. The pitch of each roof is unique. Small details like the plant pots give this picture a certain warmth.

Alexandra Cinema. Market Street. Page 66

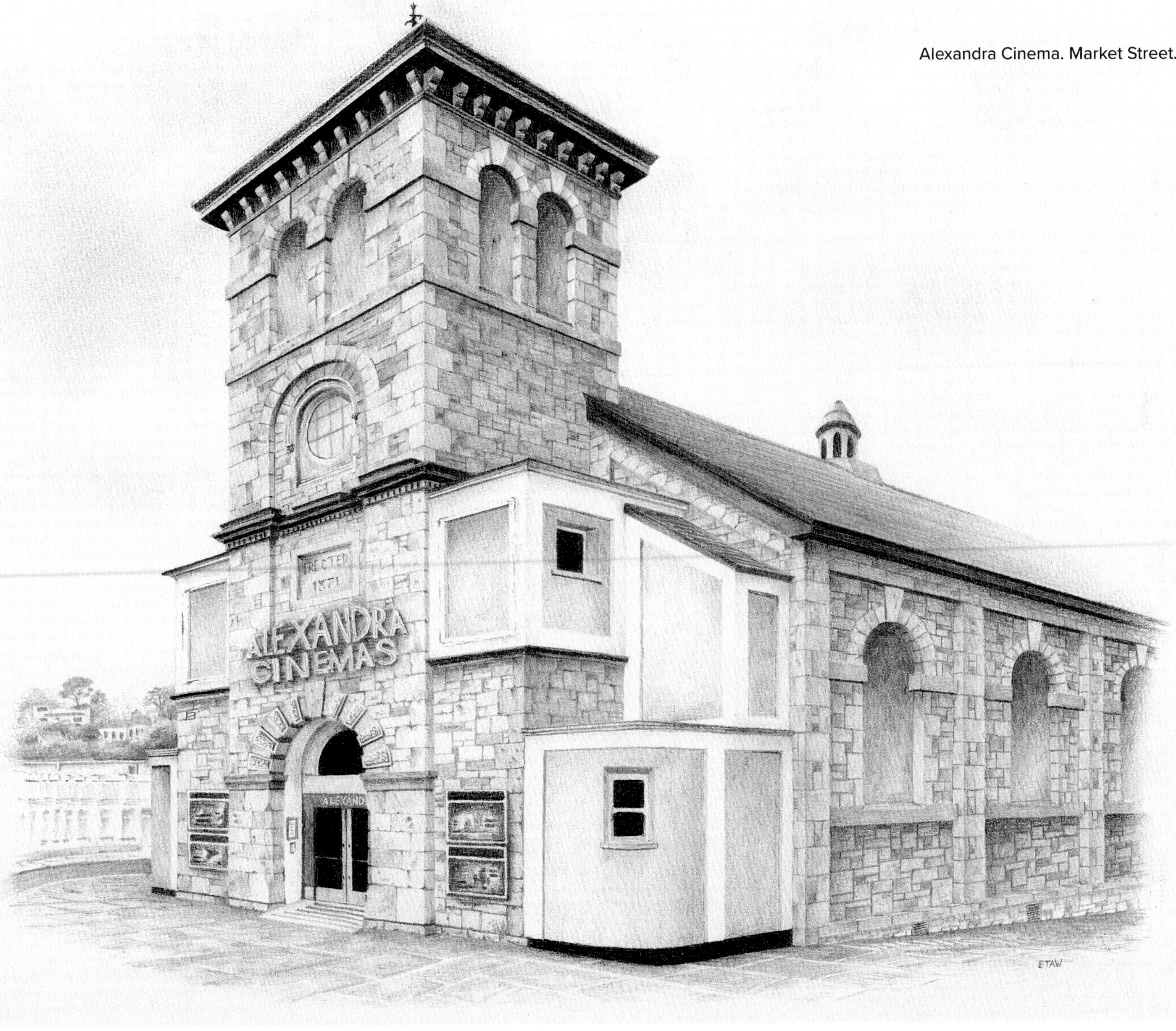
ERECTED
1871
ALEXANDRA
CINEMAS
ETAW

Union Bridge joins Wolborough parish to Highweek parish. Page 96

Passmore Edwards Building Market Street. Page 51

This was the first of the drawings and probably the most complicated. The spacing of the many windows was far from straightforward and I was able to improve my approach to this in subsequent drawings. It's definitely a building where the more you look, the more you see. Despite having photographs to work from, I still had to revisit the building itself several times to understand it. I paid special attention to the magnificent arched window on the top floor; this part of the drawing has come out particularly well.

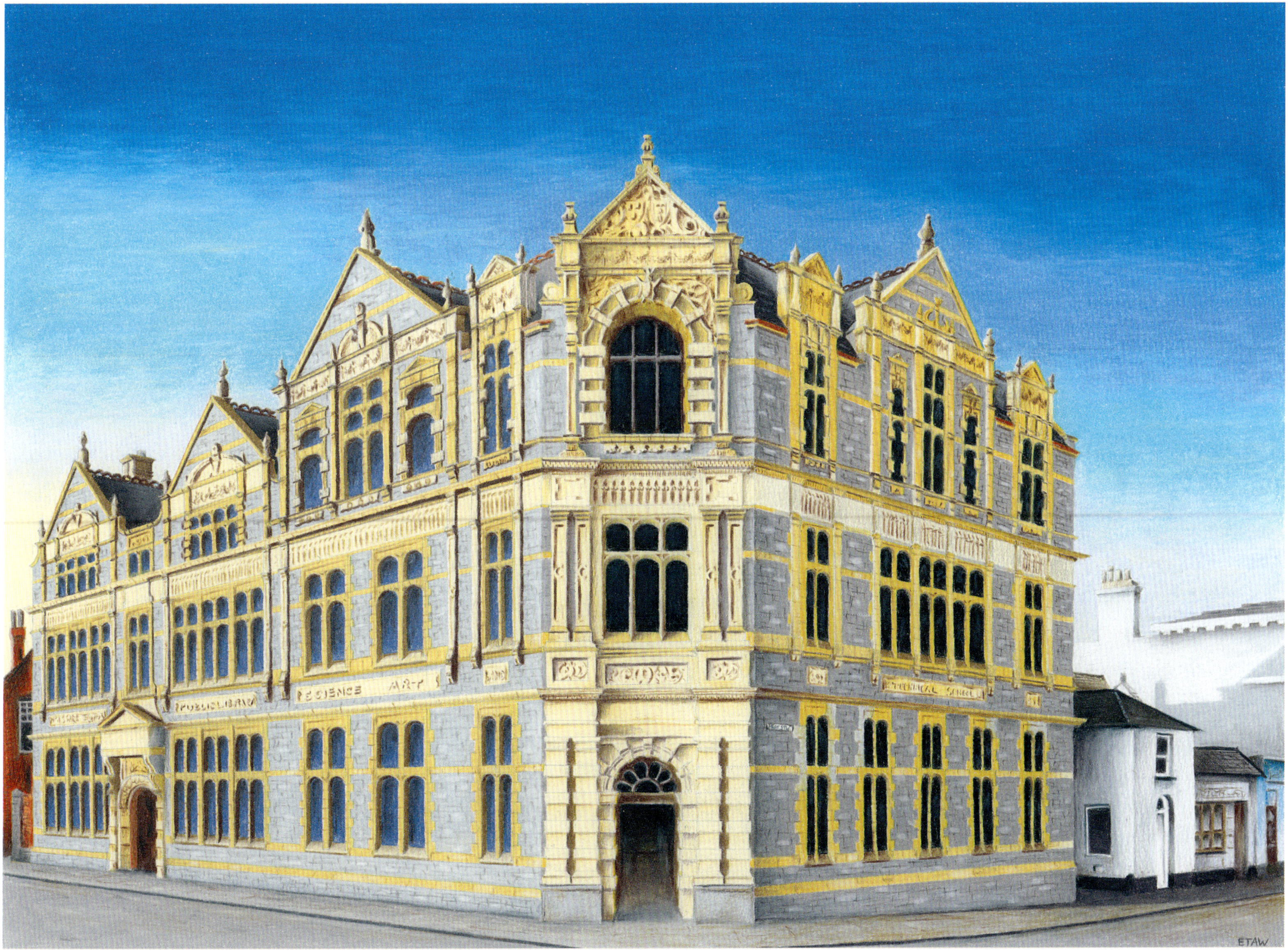
SCIENCE
ART
ETAW

Mid Devon Liberal Club in
Market Street. Page 62

ETAW

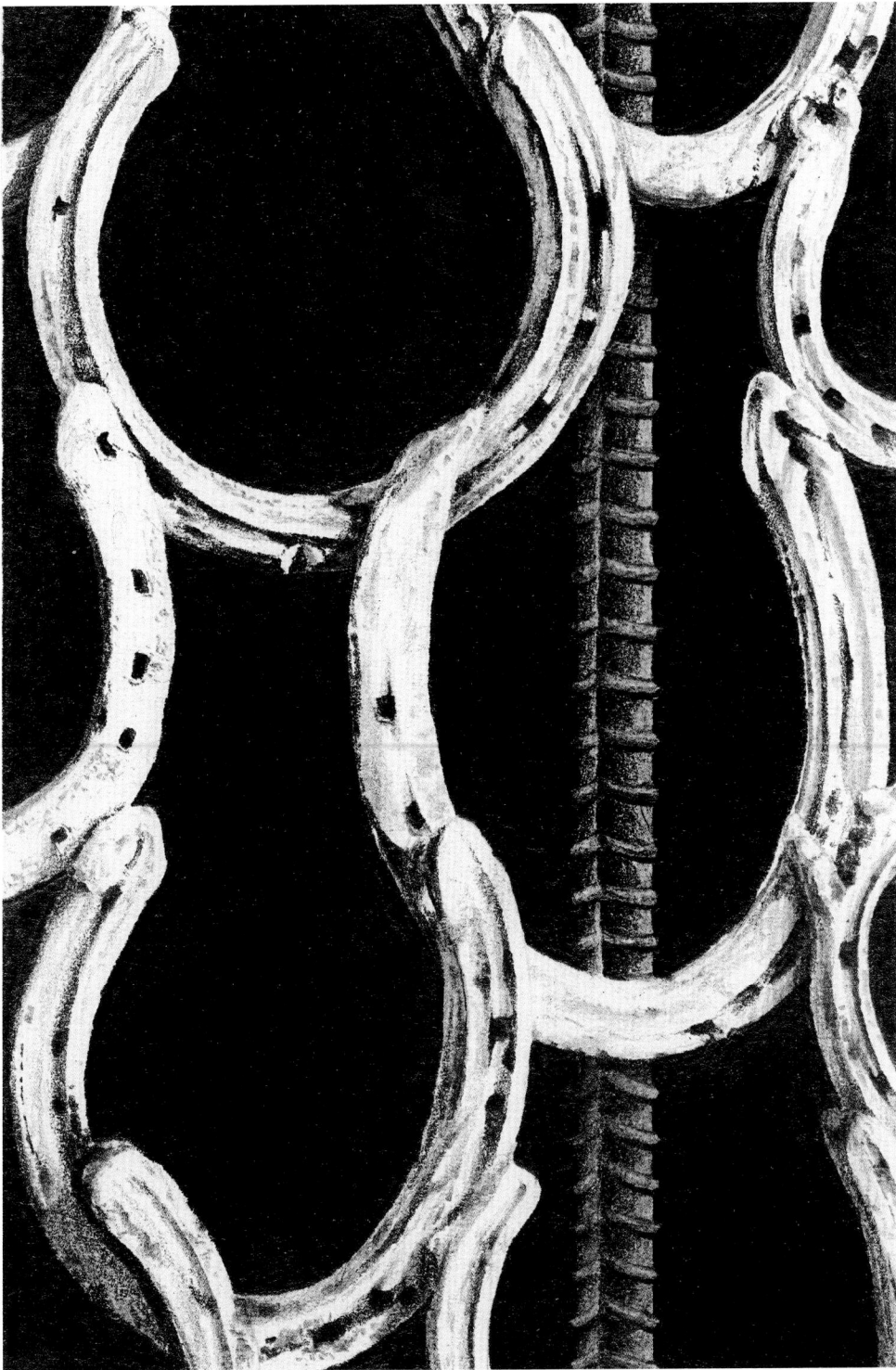

Horseshoe railings and bellcote. Union Street.
Pages 43, 46

BANK STREET

Bank Street starts at the crossroads with Courtenay, Wolborough and East Streets and today ends at the junction with Market Street opposite the Passmore Edwards Centre. In earlier times the name encompassed buildings beyond this point. Bearne's Lane runs eastwards off Bank Street and peters out in the service yard of the market square. Golden Lion Square is an urban garden on the corner of Market Street and Bank Street.

The earliest turnpike or toll road passed through Newton Bushel and Newton Abbot in 1759 and was followed by several others. They mostly formalised ancient routes taken to cross the River Lemon, and the two Newtons developed in an amphitheatre of flat land serving travellers as well as the local communities. East of this point were the treacherous Teign marshes and to the west the valley steepened. The River Lemon could be crossed here first by a ford, then by a bridge. The street was a busy thoroughfare to the markets held near St Leonard's and St. Mary's Chapels.

The road had been called Bridge Street, but it is now known as Bank Street, as the bridge was replaced in 1850 by the huge culvert that took the River Lemon underground. In September 1864 Bridge Street was officially renamed Bank Street, as it held two important banks, the Newton Bank opposite Back Lane and the Devon & Cornwall Bank near the Globe. At the same meeting in 1864 the Local Board predicted that all banks would move to Courtenay Street – and they did. There is no bank in Bank Street today.

There are four listed buildings in Bank Street.

No 4 Bank Street is a grade II listed building protected since 1972. It was built in the 1740s as a three-storey house, one room wide, over a shop. It is of painted stucco, which probably covers rough stone walls, under a slate roof. On the ground floor is a 20th century shop window and doorway. The first floor has a modern casement window, but has retained its flanking pilasters, which have moulded capitals. These support an entablature between the top of this window and the sill of the second-floor window. This upper window has the original tripartite 10/10 sash windows with painted stone mullions. The dormer window behind a panelled parapet was added some time in the 1900s. No 4 appears to have been shoehorned into the space between its neighbours as their chimneys and mouldings spread into its space.

No 4 Bank Street appears to be shoehorned into the space.

No 6 Bank Street is a grade II listed building protected since 1972. It was built in about 1860 as the Devon & Cornwall Bank in a richly ornamented Italianate style and was then considered the finest building in town; even today it competes, architecturally, with Lloyds Bank in Courtenay Street. It is of painted brick and stucco under a slate roof on four storeys and is completely symmetrical. The front is divided into three bays by four, four-part pilasters which rise from ground level to above the parapet and become simpler with height.

The ground floor has a panelled Dartmoor granite plinth which flows under and across the two doorways and shop window. The two modern doors sit in tall (stilted) arches, and the central shop window is under a shallow arch of oblong voussoirs. The first floor has four arched windows; the outer two sit under triangular pediments, and two central windows sit under one arched pediment. The second-floor windows have two cornices and shelter under a wide eave embellished with modillions. All eight windows contain original 2/2 sash windows. The top floor has a centrally placed arched dormer window.

Lloyds Bank took over the old Devon & Cornwall Bank and in 1909, when Lloyds moved into their elaborate new premises in Courtenay Street, the Post Office moved here.

No 6 Bank Street was once the finest building in town

No 7 and 9 Bank Street are grade II listed buildings protected since 1972. They are unassuming and easy to ignore, but they were built in the early 1700s and so are the oldest shops remaining from the Bridge Street days.

No 7, to the left, has painted stucco walls under a steeply pitched roof held up inside by wooden pegged beams. The front was remodelled in the 1800s and so inside a 'new' lath and plaster wall can be seen and outside is a single 3/6 window. Inside there are untouched features from the 1700s including the staircase, cupboard, mouldings, a three-pane window and panelled doors. A modern shop window has been added at street level.

No 9 is at a shallow angle to No 7 continuing the curving transition of Wolborough Street into Bank Street – perhaps to drive cattle and wagons more easily around the corner. It has more external features than No 7: a 1900s brick chimney stack, a band under the eaves, two 1800s 8/8 sash windows upstairs and a banded quoin on the right-hand side which was the end of the building until a small room was added over the carriageway. This too has an 8/8 window.

No 7 and 9 are built on a curve

No 8 and 10 are also asymmetrical. Was the missing range to the right demolished or never built?

No 12 to 16 have four moulded palm leaves and pyramids pilaster capitals are easy to miss, yet unique in Newton Abbot.

There are other interesting buildings in Bank Street.

No 17 and 19 have always been asymmetrical, although a third range to the right may have been planned. Each floor has different windows.

Golden Lion Square

The Golden Lion Inn was tucked down an unnamed alleyway with access from both Market Street and Bank Street. Built in 1623 as the Oxford Arms coaching inn, it became the Golden Lion in 1722. After blocks of buildings at Foss Corner were demolished to widen the roads, the frontage was revealed and the open space was later given a face-lift to become Golden Lion Square.

The Golden Lion's bell summoned passengers to board the departing horse-drawn coach.

In its time you could buy anything in Bank Street – from daily groceries to a new piano. Businesses came and went, through success or failure, death or retirement. There are two families who left a permanent mark on Bank Street.

John Foss had arrived in Bridge Street by 1841, selling groceries and candles from a building on the junction with Market Street that everyone called Foss Corner. John's three sons were brought into the business. The eldest, Richard, stayed at home whilst Charles and George went to the new colonies of Australia in 1882 to expand the business. Charles died there in 1884. There is a plaque in his memory in Newton's Place, Wolborough Street. George returned home in 1892 and worked with Richard. After George's death, Richard brought in his son Humphrey and began selling wines and spirits. They sold the building lease to Frank Halsé, wine merchant, in about 1919.

Newton Abbot Urban District Council bought the Foss Corner shops in 1924. Frank stayed until 1934, then moved into 1 Wolborough Street. Foss Corner was demolished in 1938 to widen the access to the market.

In 1861, 272 people lived in the 44 homes in Bank Street and two courtyards of homes named Cull's Court and White's Court. In 1881 there were 146 people living in 27 properties. Today there are 15 properties and few residents.

Bearne's Lane

The Bearne's Lane sign is made from porcelain tiles bearing white letters on a blue background and were put up in 1864 when the lane was officially named. The stones set into the lower walls are to deflect the cart, and later lorry wheels, which would otherwise damage the building.

If you were to plot the original Bearne's Lane on a modern map it would run from Bank Street in a straight line to the service yard near Lloyds Bank market entrance. Almost all of the buildings have disappeared, but it was once a busy lane with a coal yard, timber yard, stores and houses, all occupied by the Bearne family and their tenants.

In 1843 Andrew Bearne was a grocer and timber and coal merchant; by 1862 his son James ran a grocery shop with a coal yard at Jetty Marsh quay and at Teignbridge on the Stover Canal. By 1893 James's son, John, was concentrating on the coal business. Between 1808 and 2009, 71 members of the wider Bearne family were buried in Highweek All Saint's graveyard, with others in St Mary's Churchyard, Wolborough.

COURTENAY STREET

Courtenay Street is named after William Courtenay, the Earl of Devon, and runs from the Globe Hotel (Austins) to the middle of Hero Bridge over the River Lemon, where the parish boundaries of Wolborough and Highweek meet.

There are six listed buildings in Courtenay Street, but others are also worth noticing.

No 1 Courtenay Street, the Globe Hotel, now part of Austins, is on the corner of Bank Street. It is a grade II listed building, protected since 1949. The original Globe Hotel was well placed at the junction of Courtenay Street with Bank Street (formerly Bridge Street), East Street and Wolborough Street, where three turnpike roads had met since 1762. Horse-drawn coaches travelling between Exeter, Torquay and Plymouth could stop here for fresh horses and the passengers were served with food and drink. Thomas Palk kept the Globe from 1789 to his death in 1803. The new landlord was John Beazley, who served his customers for the next 43 years. When he died on 30 October 1846, just months before the opening ceremony of Newton Station, he was described as 'highly esteemed by all classes'. His son, also named John, took over as landlord but only lived until 1854.

The Globe Hotel's entrance moved from Bank Street to Courtenay Street.

The Newton Abbot Improvement Act of 1836 enabled a road to be made from the Globe Inn to join up with the Totnes Bridgetown and Pomeroy Turnpike Trustees' road being built from Kingsteignton to Newton Abbot. The roads would meet at Hero Bridge. The Earl of Devon and the Duke of Somerset, as major landowners and beneficiaries, put up most of the money, but the remainder was raised through voluntary subscriptions from the townsfolk. The road was completed in 1842 and called Courtenay Street. The Globe Hotel was rearranged so that a new and impressive entrance faced this new street. The *Western Times* reported on 23 September 1843 that the new hotel occupied a considerable frontage in Courtenay Street and is 'imposing by its size, elegance and proportions, and no expense had been spared in its interior'. In celebration, the Earl held 'a choice and costly dinner' for 130 of the local wealthy and influential people,

The Globe's entrance has four granite columns and two pilasters.

many of whom had subscribed to the new road.

The building's new entrance has four plain but solid Tuscan columns, hewn from the local Dartmoor granite, with two granite pilasters attached to the wall behind them. An elaborate cast-iron railing creates a first-floor balcony, which has been used over the years to announce election results and watch the rising floodwaters. The old entrance, with its simple cast-iron balcony above, can be seen in Bank Street.

The hotel has twenty sash windows on the upper two floors, and in the Assembly Room extension, where dances, dinners and meetings were held, there are four beautiful arched sash windows above the modern shop fronts.

Inside is an open-well staircase with cast-iron balusters supporting a mahogany handrail which led to the bedrooms.

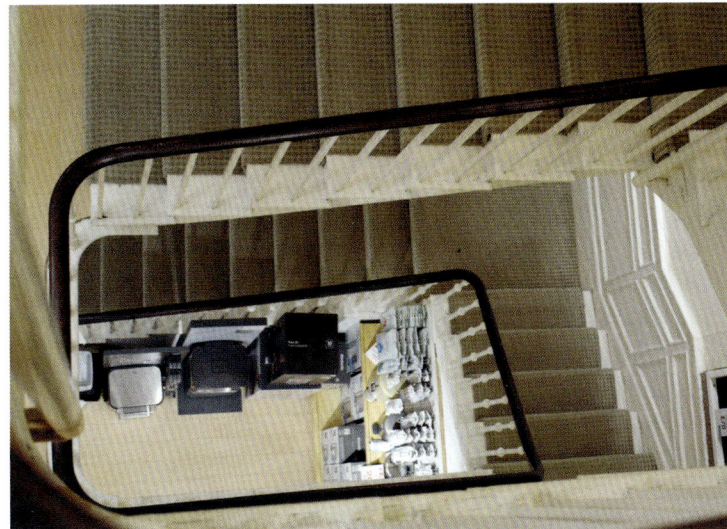

The four arched windows of the Assembly Room now sit above shops.

Austins has a vertiginous open-well staircase. The balusters became simpler as you climbed up to the old hotel's staff quarters.

No 2 and 4 Courtenay Street, part of Austins stores, are on the corner of East Street. They are grade II listed buildings, protected since 1972. The two four-storey buildings are opposite The Globe, and curve around their prominent corner site. They were built in 1844 as part of the Courtenay Street development. In 1851 No 2 was Philip Michelmore's drapers' shop. He, his wife, their five children, eight staff and some servants and his mother-in-law, all lived above the shop. In 1904 it was a bank. Next door, at No 4 Courtenay Street the 1851 occupants were Edward Sluman, a printer, and his wife.

Flanking the former corner doorway to No 2 are two fluted Doric columns, hand-hewn from Dartmoor granite. The entrance to No 4 has two more columns between bay windows with decorative ironwork.

The doorways of No 2 and 4 have fluted granite columns on an imposing corner site.

No 4 Courtenay Street has decorative ironwork below and above the window sill.

Viewed from Wolborough Street, this building has single or paired pilasters rising from the ground floor, spanning the first and second floors, to the third floor. Anything which spans several floors is termed giant-order. Dividing the second and third floors is a wide cornice. All three upper floors have sash windows, some framed by eared architraves — small plaster panels which stick out from the windows like ears. Some windows in Queen Street have knee architraves.

Austins was opened in 1924 by Charles Ernest Austin, who was born in 1898 in Suffolk, the son of a draper. In the First World War, as Lieutenant C.E. Austin of The King's Royal Rifle Corps, he was awarded the Military Cross (MC) for his conspicuous gallantry and devotion to duty on the Western Front, in attacking German trenches at Mericourt without losing a man. During the Second World War Charles Austin combined the responsibilities of running his shop with service in the Home Guard and as an air raid warden. His son, Ernest, was a pilot in the war and was killed in action over northern France in 1943. Charles Ernest Austin, MC died in 1998 aged 100.

A spring 2020 view down Courtenay Street

The former Marks & Spencer's shop has four giant-order pilasters, and dentils under the overhanging roof.

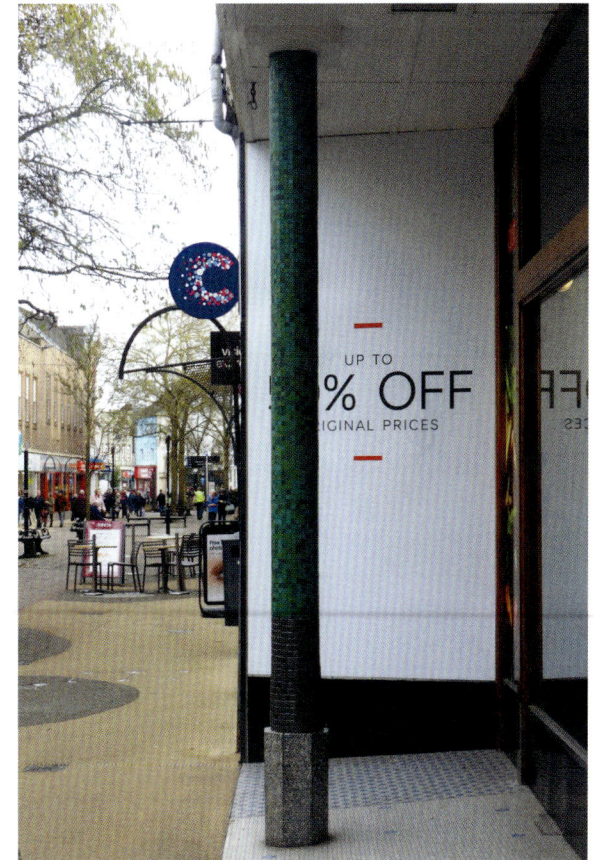

This odd column sits in the shop doorway of the former M&S shop.

Between Austins and the next two listed buildings is an interesting building which is not listed. For a long time it was occupied by Marks & Spencer.

The first and second floors are spanned by four giant-order pilasters, with stylised capitals on top, under the overhanging roof are square dentils that look like a row of teeth. The aprons between four of the six windows have a central diamond shape.

The wide entrance to this building has a well-laid mosaic floor in blue and white tiles. Sitting on this is a singular oddity: a curious, circular column clad in green, blue and grey mosaic tiles on an octagonal granite-looking composite base. There is nothing else like it in Newton Abbot.

No 12 and 14 Courtenay Street, two matching shops on the south side of the street, are grade II listed buildings, protected since 1996.

These two imposing Italianate, three-storey shops with flats above were built in the 1840s and form a prominent part of the local streetscape.

Each symmetrical building has two sash windows. They are in three parts (tripartite), with timber mullions dividing them. Three of the four windows have curled consoles at the top of the mullions. The second-floor windows have panelled aprons underneath. Four giant-order, Tuscan pilasters flank the windows and support two triangular pediments.

In 1851, No 12 was the home and draughting office of the Earl of Devon's surveyor and architect, Humphrey Abberley. He lived here with his wife, five daughters and a servant, but he also had an office in Teignmouth. Abberley drew up the first plans for the 'metropolis of villas' on Wolborough Hill, Courtenay Park and Devon Square and devised the town's first flood-prevention plans in 1854 but died in 1855 before the work was finished. His role was taken by Joseph W. Rowell.

In 1908, the Town Hall was in Courtenay Street. On 18 January, there were 12,000 people standing outside to hear the result of a local by-election. When the result was read out, it was not as predicted! A considerable riot erupted between the supporters, which spilled into Union Street, where most of the action happened — and most damage was done — stirred up by the presence of suffragette, Emmeline Pankhurst.

A pair of houses at No 12 & 14 now have shops at street level.

No 44 Courtenay Street is Gerry & Co., Jewellers.

Frederick William Gerry was born in Torquay in 1856. By the age of 25 he was established at 44 Courtenay Street as a watchmaker and jeweller. When he died in 1937, after 56 years of trading at this address, his obituary listed his work in the Liberal Party, Newton Abbot Urban District Council and the Higher Education Committee, and his active interest in arts and crafts, photography, Dartmoor and local sport. He was the man to go to if you needed a new trophy made, a presentation clock, a wedding canteen of cutlery, as well as your watch repaired or a bit of cash for the old silverware.

Being close to the entrance to the market may have given Mr Gerry some trade, but in 1899 he had an unwanted customer. A bullock escaped from the market and entered his shop. No doubt his assistants waved and shouted at the beast until it was scared off — but it broke the glass shade and mantle of the shop's gas light as it left.

Gerry's coat of arms includes a bishop, a knight's helm, a set of scales, a lion's head and two unicorns hung with a ring and a timer, with the banner motto, like the Rothchild's, which means Harmony, Integrity, Industry.

Gerry's is the oldest firm still trading in Courtenay Street and sells traditional wares and makes repairs.

The impressive Lloyds Bank on Drum Clock Corner, was built in 1908 and is a grade II listed building.

No 41 Courtenay Street, Lloyds Bank on Drum Clock Corner is a grade II listed building, protected since 1983.

Drum Clock Corner had long been a meeting place for people, and a frequent venue for the bands that played around the town. It was also where innumerable accidents happened as the then narrow access road led to the market. The old corner building was owned by solicitors Baker, Watts, Alsop and Woollcombe. Lloyds Bank bought their building for £7,000 in 1907 and demolished it for £89. The new Lloyds Bank and Chambers was to be set 24 feet further back to create a wider access. It was built in 1908 for £10,000 by contractors Sapcote and Sons of Birmingham in an Edwardian Baroque style to a design by Rowell, Son and Locke, architects of Devon Square, now known as LSN.

Lloyds Bank is an elaborate building with splendid proportions and perfect lines. The pale Beer stone is shown off by the squared red Poltimore sandstone, and the building rests on a plinth of Dartmoor granite, giving the whole building the solidity any bank would like to portray. The Drum Clock was transferred from the original building to the current one and so is the oldest part of this building.

The main building has three storeys. On the ground floor are large plate-glass windows, adorned with 24 fluted stone pilasters with the carved foliage of a Corinthian top.

The first and second floors are spanned by 21 giant-order, fluted Corinthian pilasters. The first-floor windows sit under semicircular or triangular pediments, whereas the second-floor window surrounds have alternating block work and three keystones at the top.

The Drum Clock above the entrance to Lloyds Bank

The two massive doorways of Lloyds Bank face the market and Courtenay Street. They are imposing and elaborately carved with open pediments which hold the coat of arms and emblems of the bank – to catch the eye of the passer-by.

The Corinthian style pilasters flank the windows.

Lloyds Bank has giant-order Corinthian pilasters and three different window shapes.

There is a stone balustraded parapet around the roof over dentil mouldings. A semicircular recess holds the projecting Drum Clock and the other corner has a circular oculus window. The stone was carved by sculptors James Carwardine of Exeter and James Beaman Hunt of Plymouth, including the beehive, representing industry and hard work, with 'EST 1765' showing when Lloyds Bank started as the Taylor and Lloyd private bank.

Inside there is the same exuberance with egg-and-dart moulded dado rails, elaborate plaster ceilings, Corinthian columns and carved wood door surrounds — repeating the beehive motif.

It is a truly a magnificent building!

Lloyds was established in 1765 by Taylor and Lloyd in Birmingham and adopted the beehive as a symbol of industry and hard work.

No 47 Courtenay Street, Invertère Buildings is important, but unlisted, so unprotected by legislation. It is next to the Lloyds Chambers entrance.

Invertère is Latin for 'to turn about' and describes a reversible coat, warm and rainproof. The tailor William Parkin, had become agent for the Hewlett Invertère coat in Bratton Fleming and his brothers, Alfred and Arthur Parkin, came to Newton Abbot to make and sell the coats from this building from 1907 to 1939. Arthur's son, Harold, joined them and coats continued to be made here until the business was sold in 1948. At the time of writing, the Invertère Coat Company Ltd still has a presence in Newton Abbot.

Invertère Buildings is made from ashlar blocks — squared limestone, with a red brick band which rises and arches over the four mirror-paired windows on the first floor. A stone drip moulding runs above them to deflect the rain. In the distinctively shaped Dutch gable is a dark green and cream tile name panel which has a wonderful Green Man motif with long curling foliage coming from his mouth. Above this is an inset diamond panel with a brick surround. So much to see in such a small space.

There are other Dutch gables on houses in Courtenay Park.

On census night in 1851, there were 157 people living in 34 buildings in Courtenay Street. Most of their jobs are recognisable, but some might be a bit out of place in Courtenay Street today: Philip Webber, iron founder, Thomas Ruby, coachbuilder and wheelwright, Thomas Shobbrook, blacksmith, and Thomas Martin, master tornographer who engraved the Lord's Prayer onto a silver sixpence for the Great Exhibition of 1851. By 1911 there were 106 people living in Courtenay Street, including three florists.

The curved and pointed Dutch gable of the Invertère Buildings

The Invertère Buildings' name and green man are in hand-crafted tiles.

UNION STREET

Union Street starts at the junction with Courtenay Street and ends at the junction with East Street. Off to the right is Carlisle Street and Summerland Cottages, once known as Summerland Place, and off to the left is School Road.

Acting as agent and architect for the Earl of Devon, Joseph W. Rowell first mooted a new road from Courtenay Street to East Street in 1874 to release land for building. Demolition of the Newfoundland Inn on East Street was considered, but eventually permission was given to join School Road, which already exited onto East Street. The new road took the name of Union Street as it led to the gates of the Newton Abbot Union Workhouse. This had been built in 1839 to accept the poor and sick of a union of 39 local parishes and was funded by a rate levied on the residents of those parishes and by charitable donations.

Work to build Union Street began in Courtenay Street in 1885 where two very imposing shops flanked the new road entrance. Completed in 1886 they were built for Charles Pope, tailor, hatter and outfitter, and for Lawrence Stockman, draper. Designed by Joseph W. Rowell they wrapped around the corners and were described as 'lofty, commodious and rich in architectural design'. No 40 Courtenay Street was demolished and Barclays Bank, designed by Deacon, Knight & Granger of London,

was built in 1961. The design included the unique street sign for Union Street carved in the stone. No 42 became the Midland Bank now HSBC, and was extensively 'blandified', with only some gable detail and dentils under the roof remaining.

There are no listed buildings in Union Street. From the outset it was occupied by clubs, offices, shops and houses. From the mid-1920s many of the houses were converted into shops, but there were enough families here in 1939–1940 to give homes to 15 refugees. There are many unifying features across the two- and three-storey buildings. They are built from cream brick with red brick detailing in bands across the fronts, around chimney stacks and around windows and gables. There are bargeboards fretted with quatrefoils with deep eaves supported by brackets. At most doorways and property boundaries there are pilasters with a fluted band at the top under a 'bird-box' capital. Unfortunately, as though an afterthought, there is a complex liana-like tangle of gutters, downpipes and pavement gullies on most of the buildings and to affix these there has been some damage to the fronts.

Elaborately banded brickwork and fretted bargeboards on the gable above Gunter's shop.

No 1 Union Street was built for the Mid Devon Liberal Club and opened in 1887, as a new three-storey building with a lecture room to seat 150 people and an election agent's office, where Edwin Perry and others worked on campaigns for Sir Charles Seale-Hayne, Harold Eve and Charles Buxton. It is brick-built with five arched windows on the upper two storeys and a central bay window over a once impressive doorway, now replaced. There may be coloured brick detailing on the front wall, but it has been painted over.

Opposite the Mid Devon Liberal Club, at No 8 Union Street, is the Mid Devon Constitutional Club. It can be seen from Courtenay Street as it sits on the bend in the road. Designed by Joseph W. Rowell, the foundation stone was laid in 1887 by

The Mid Devon Constitutional Club has lost the ground floor detailing.

the Earl of Devon and the new Leader of the House of Commons, William Henry Smith, better known as W. H. Smith, bookseller and newsagent. He had been elected as a Member of Parliament in 1868, and was the First Lord of the Admiralty, twice Secretary of State for War, and later First Lord of the Treasury. The three-storey 'Con Club' had fourteen arched windows to the front with a central door under a semicircular, balustraded balcony. The ground-floor frontage was remodelled, and the detail erased.

The members had the benefit of a library, a reading room and smoking, lecture and billiard rooms, with the services of an on-site caretaker who was also the billiard marker. The Earl of Devon and Sir Michael Hicks-Beach, President of the Board of Trade, officially opened the club in 1888 followed by a luncheon for 250 people in the Alexandra Hall.

It was the proximity of these two rival political parties that created the flashpoint in 1908 which ended in rioting, injury and death. The Liberals had held the Mid Devon constituency for years, and when a by-election was called the Liberal party's candidate, Charles Buxton, was expected to win against the Conservatives' Captain Morrison-Bell. An estimated 12,000 to 15,000 supporters, with their party flags and rosettes, assembled in front of the Market Hall, where the votes were being counted, and spread into Courtenay Street, Union Street and East Street. When the result was declared, the Liberals had lost the seat. There was uproar. The results were posted at the Town Hall in Courtenay Street and carried to the two clubs. The sound of the cheering inside the Constitutional Club enraged the Liberals outside and the stone-throwing began.

Coming into Courtenay Street from Queen Street were suffragettes Mrs Emmeline Pankhurst, her daughter Sylvia and her friend Mrs Nellie Martell. They had come to support the Conservatives, who advocated votes for women. When the Liberal supporters recognised Mrs Pankhurst, their anger had another focus. She was pelted with eggs and had to shelter in Mr Banbury's County Stores on Hopkins Lane. The ruffians broke down the gate to the yard, cornered the women and knocked them down into the mud. The feisty ladies beat off the unruly crowd with their umbrellas! They were eventually rescued by the police, who had commandeered Harry Balls and a car from his new garage in The Avenue, now Balls Corner.

The Liberal supporters had taken possession of Union Street and 100 police had arrived on horseback and foot to control and disperse the pushing and jeering crowd. Two magistrates were requested to attend to read the Riot Act before arrests could be made, but the men had their women and children with them, so the police stayed back. At the end of the night, one policeman had suffered concussion, and supporters from both sides were bruised and battered. All of the windows, front and back, of the Mid Devon Constitutional Club were smashed. The following day the dead body of staunch Conservative, ex-Royal Marine Henry Rendell, was found in the mill stream with severe head injuries. The next election was a much more sedate affair.

Other occupants of the Union Street houses have been decorators, coal merchants and a chimney sweep. The shops have been saddlers, basket makers, tailors, boot makers, hairdressers, a cycle manufacturer and a baker. The offices over the years included the Inland Revenue and Surveyor of Taxes, and lots of solicitors.

No 2 Union Street had a notable resident in Thomas Coombe, harness maker and saddler and his sons Leonard, who took over the business, and Rueben, who joined the Royal Army Medical Corps in 1914. He wrote harrowing letters home about being at the front. Leonard Coombe became an urban district councillor then Chairman of the Council in 1935/6 and county councillor, until his death in 1937. After 160 years in the trade, the Coombe name can still be seen on the equestrian and saddlery shop at No 13 Highweek Street.

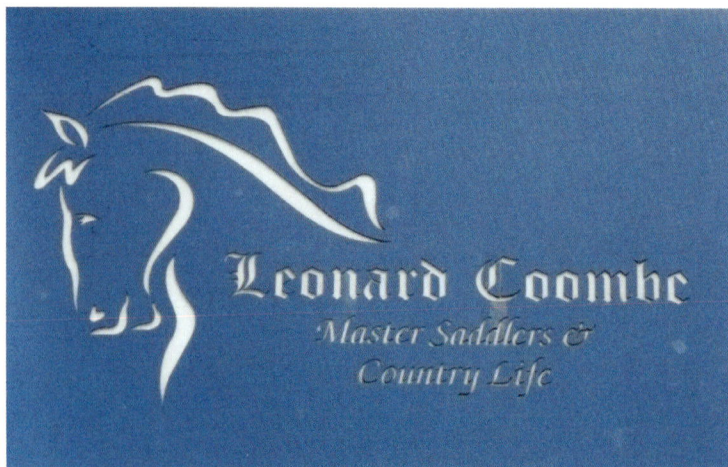

Leonard Coombe's shop was at No 2 Union Street, but is now in Highweek Street.

No 13 Union Street, Günter Watchmakers, has a modish 1960s-style shop front with small black glazed tiles stacked below a broad stainless-steel window frame. The door handle is a bold pair of steel clock hands and the G of Günter is a clock face. Günther von Waskowski arrived from East Prussia in 1955, established his business in Wolborough Street, and bought No 13 in 1965. His meticulously kept ledgers, full of detail and symbols, told him when customers had last had their timepieces cleaned or repaired. He was Chairman then Vice-President of the Chamber of Trade and was a founding member, then Life President of the Twinning Association linking Newton Abbot with Besigheim and Ay. Günther von Waskowski died in 2011, aged 90, but the business remains under his name. There is a seat in Golden Lion Square as a reminder of his work for the town.

Carlisle Street and Summerland Cottages

Between No 14 and 16 Union Street is a road which was once called Summerland Street, now Carlisle Street and Summerland Cottages, which goes through to East Street. As a reverse to Union Street these cottages were built in red brick with cream detailing. The 13 cottages had 49 residents in 1911, working as dressmaker, tailor, warehouseman, schoolteacher, porter, charwoman, bargeman, baker, police constable, house painter, boot maker, gardener, two workers at Vicary's wool mill, and an agricultural machinist possibly at Henry Beares foundry.

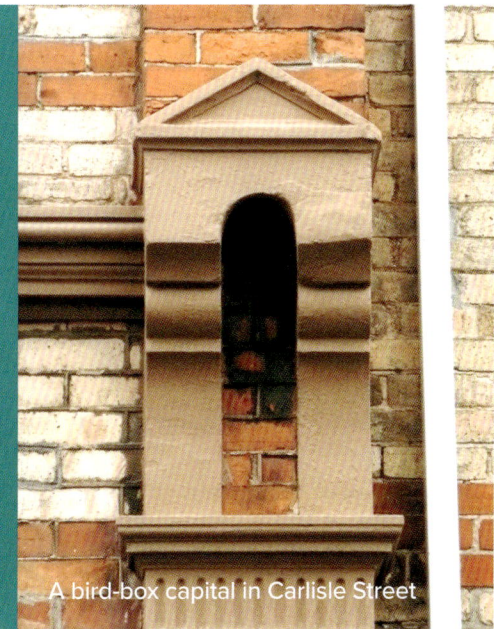

A bird-box capital in Carlisle Street

No 17 and 19 on the corner of Union Street and School Road were built as the County Police Station and residence for Sergeant Nicholls by F. A.A. Stacey in 1886 and has a nice date stone in the gable. The police cells can still be seen inside. In 1902 it was Sergeants William Coles and John Creech sharing the job in charge of seven constables, and in 1932 it was Sergeant Gale who had the surprise of opening the door one evening to Prince George. The prince had flown his plane to Plymouth and was driven to various engagements in a car flying the Royal Standard. After his last visit to Seale-Hayne Agricultural College he was due to fly out from Haldon aerodrome, but fog descended, and he was to catch a train instead. As there was a long wait, his equerry took him to the nearest safe place – Newton Abbot Police Station. When the prince strolled in Sergeant Gale swiftly found him a comfortable seat rather than the bench used by prisoners. The fancy car flying a flag drew a crowd and the Prince was cheered as he was driven away. At some stage the artistic horseshoe railings were installed at No 19, but this building was never occupied by a shoeing smith, a welder nor a registry office.

The 1886 datestone in the eaves of the former Police Station

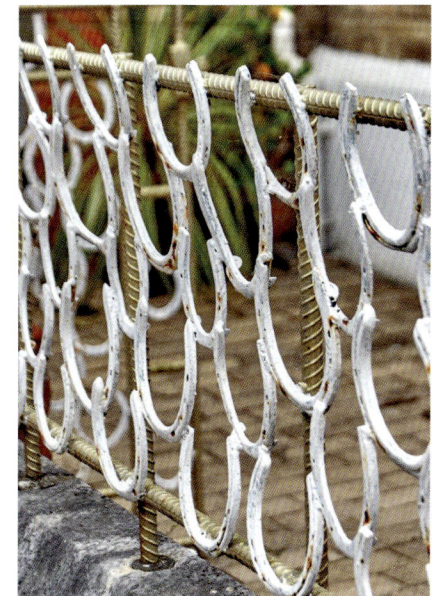

Horseshoe railings secure the old Police Station

No 22 was occupied by solicitor John Pidsley who had set up practice here in early 1890. He was joined by his son and then Norman Roberts to become Pidsley & Roberts. By 1985 No 20 had internal links to No 22. Bartlett's chartered accountants bought the buildings in 2009.

No 24 and 26 were the offices of Samuel Segar from at least 1904. His family home was Ringslade Farm and his family's gravestones in All Saints' Church, Highweek, go back to the mid-1600s. Samuel trained as an architect and was appointed surveyor, sanitary inspector and engineer for Newton Abbot's rural parishes in 1880. In these parishes he also gained commissions to design buildings, one of the earliest being for Charles Seale-Hayne at Pitt House, Chudleigh in 1888. As work increased, he took an apprentice and then this office in Union Street, keeping a family home at 37 Devon Square. In Newton Abbot he worked on specialised buildings for the Union Workhouse, the Vicary tannery and woollen mills, Fairweather's Commercial Hotel, the new hospital in East Street, the isolation hospital at Ogwell Cross, the Co-Op Bakery in King Street – all but the latter have been demolished. All four of Samuel's sons served in the First World War, Frank Evans Segar, receiving the Military Cross. When Samuel died in 1925, Frank took his job, and his offices, until his death in 1959.

No 30 was built as a Plymouth Brethren Gospel Chapel and Sunday School, which seated 250 people to listen to talks on the gospels and missionary work, and for wedding and funeral services. In 1901 the Salvation Army was renting a room in the Alexandra Hall and bought the Gospel Hall and a house next door for £700 as permanent premises. The Plymouth Brethren took over Prospect Chapel in East Street, now demolished. An extensive refurbishment of the Salvation Army Hall in 1940 was opened by Lord Mamhead.

School Road

School Road was built before Union Street. The row of eleven cottages was once called Bridford Terrace, built on one of the Earl of Devon's orchards. In about 1891 builder Hugh Mills bought two of the Bridford Terrace cottages, demolished No 5 and rebuilt the two exposed walls in Kingsteignton brick. He went to this expense to gain access to the large plot of land behind, which he leased from the Earl of Devon and set up a builder's yard with a workshop, office and stores. Newton Abbot Urban District Council took the lease from Hugh Mills for nine years until 1904. In 1911 there were 32 occupants in Bridford Terrace – five in the building trade, a schoolteacher, a workhouse laundress, three tailors, a pottery mill worker and a hotel ostler.

Hopkins Court is off School Road and here the architects have faithfully mirrored the use of banded bricks prevalent in Union Street and beyond, in a considered design that is visually attractive and structurally interesting. On the wall facing School Road is a piece of art commissioned from Peter Osborne who has created a sculpture which captures the historic elements associated with the nearby ropewalk, built by Samuel Yeo in 1828, and the

Peter Osborne's ship, harpoon and rope sculpture

Newfoundland fishing trade – ship, harpoon and rope.

At the end of the School Road cottages is a two-storey building with a front wall of ashlar limestone with brick and stone detailing around the ground- and first-floor windows, the gable vent and the off-centre door. Underneath the upper windowsill is a small engraved stone recording the use of this solid little building as 'Wolborough Parish Room and Soup Kitchen'. It was built in 1869/70 near the entrance to the Union Workhouse

Wolborough Parish Room and Soup Kitchen is now part of Wolborough School (left). The engraved stone plaque under the window.

in East Street and used to cook food and care for the sick and the poor – maybe for those who really did not want to go into the Workhouse. Early users of the Wolborough Parish Room for regular meetings were the Oddfellows' Lodge. The building is now incorporated into Wolborough School and an engraved stone inside extends the story. It reads 'The freehold of this building was purchased in 1908 by Mrs Henry Jacob née Hatch in memory of the Rev. Henry Tudor, rector of Wolborough with whom she started the Wolborough Sick and Soup Kitchen in 1867.' Sophia Hatch had married stationer Henry Jacobs in 1851 and she and the Reverend Tudor raised funds by public subscription and bazaars to run a temporary soup kitchen before this building was erected. Tudor Road, off East Street was named after this hard-working Reverend.

The last building in Union Street was built as a National School, one of many started around the country by the National Society for Promoting Religious Education to 'provide elementary Church of England education to the children of the poor'. In 1865 the Wolborough parish National School was housed in a dark, cramped two-roomed building in East Street, later converted to the town's first Armoury. Joseph Soper, a retired fish and fish oil merchant of Powderham Villa in Courtenay Park, offered the Rev. Tudor £50 to spend on church business. The good reverend took Mr Soper to the old National School and asked whether the money could be spent on a new school instead. Other local people gave money to the building fund and the new school was built in 1870 employing a schoolmistress for £50 p.a. In 1877 there were 800 Wolborough School children with the rector, teachers and friends on what

Wolborough School's cream stone bellcote has the bell and chain pull

had become an annual treat to Stover Park given by the Duke of Somerset. A special train with fourteen carriages had been arranged by Mr Pratt, the station master to get them all to Heathfield Station and back.

With the increasing population of Wolborough, the school was enlarged in 1893 for an intake of 460 children and a few years later headmaster John Knott and headmistress Miss Acland had an average attendance of 255 boys and 256 girls. 1940 brought reorganisation. Wolborough School would be for children under 10 years old only. Older girls were to go to the new Wain Lane School and boys to Highweek Road Senior School.

Despite the many additions to the layout, the school buildings have a nice mix of limestone, with red brick detailing and some cream stonework. The boundary walls are random limestone with stepped pyramid capstones to the gateposts making the whole campus feel solid.

Limestone walls of Wolborough Church of England Nursery and Primary School

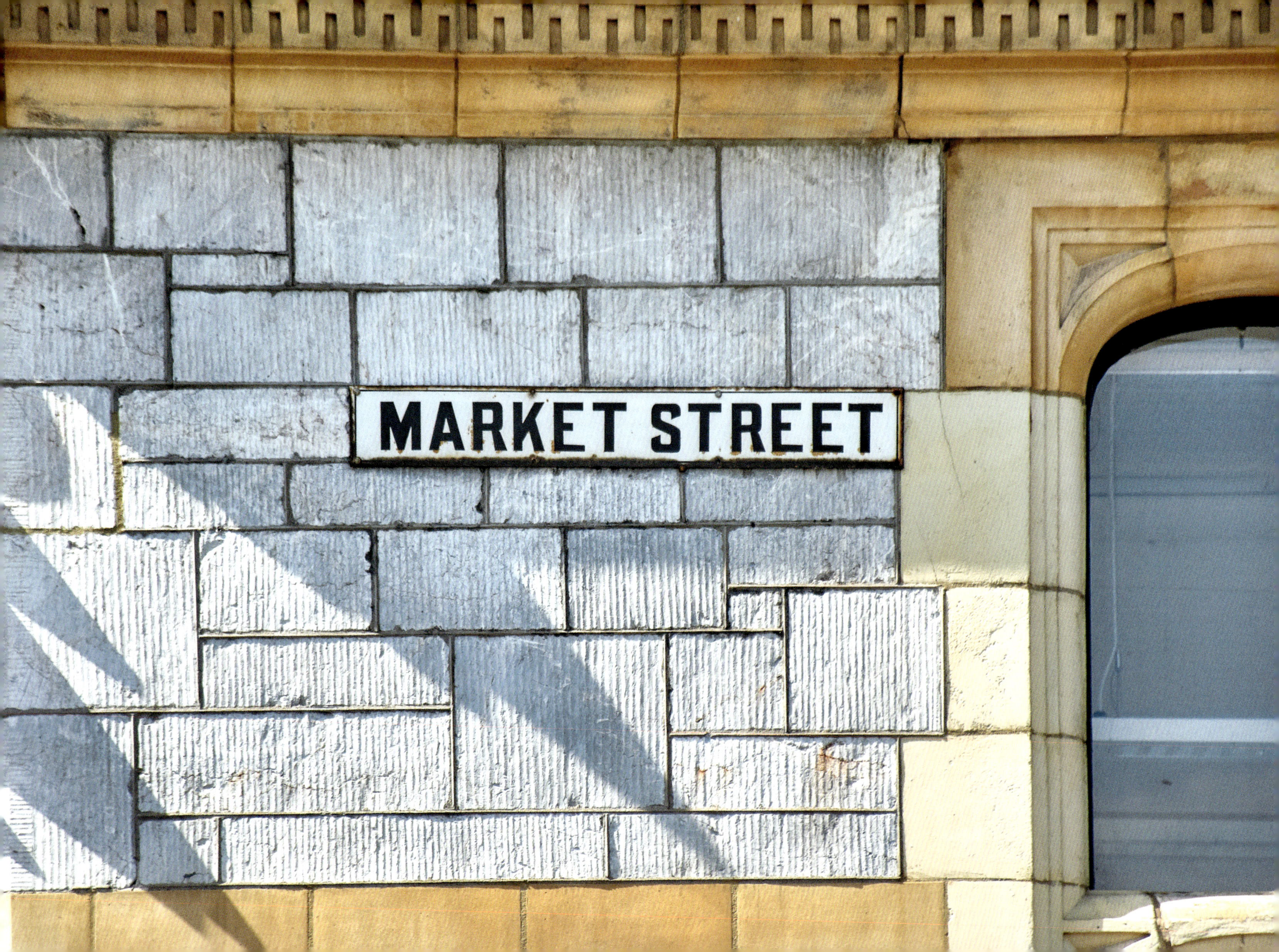
MARKET STREET

Market Street was once known as Market Terrace as it only had houses on the north side. Not surprisingly it leads to the livestock, indoor and outdoor market areas. It starts at the junction with Bank Street and Highweek Street, and ends at the junction with Sherborne Road, now used by buses. Sherborne Road ends at the junction with Kingsteignton Road, which itself ends, surprisingly, at the parish boundary with Teigngrace.

Markets and fairs had been held around Newton Abbot's St. Leonard's Chapel and Newton Bushel's St. Mary's Chapel since the 1200s under the control of the lords of the two manors. The two markets merged in 1633 and activity focussed on the larger space around the Chapel of St Leonard in Wolborough Street. In 1823 the old market hall in Wolborough Street was demolished to widen the turnpike road. The lord of the manor, Reverend Richard Lane, then moved the market to the present area in 1825–6 creating Market Street and erecting the first market buildings here. He sold the market to

Wolborough Local Board in 1864 for £8,000 and the pannier market and Corn Exchange/Alexandra Hall were built in 1871, but there have been many refinements to the street and the markets since then.

The roads and bridges into the market were always congested on market and fair days, with farmers and tradesmen buying and selling, and entertainers working the crowds. Adding to the melee, the 1881 census enumerator recorded two caravans parked up, belonging to horse dealers Moses Small and his son Henry.

In this short street were three public houses and a coffee tavern. In 1901 Henry Walling kept the Golden Lion; Mary Short ran the Market House Inn, now the Market Gate; Samuel Lang ran the Bradley Hotel, now the Jolly Farmer and Sydney Grice ran the Dolphin Coffee House. All public houses in town had a slaughterhouse at the back as there were no abattoirs or butcher's shops, and they had stabling for the market goers' horses and carts, with tying rings on the walls. There were numerous complaints about animals being left unattended while the

owners' were in pubs, including a farmer who had brought his two-year-old to market and left her in the straw with the sheep he had just bought.

The residents of the street paid solicitor Sidney Hacker, a fellow occupier, to write to Wolborough Local Board in December 1893 about the nuisance of the recent September fair. He listed damage to property, hindrance to their businesses, obstruction and smoke from six gypsy caravans horse trading, noise from the steam merry-go-round, shows and shooting galleries, and the mess left behind. The 1894 fair was held on the athletic ground near Queen Street.

These residents may have been saved from that September fair, but they were caught by the November flood. Market Street is built over the River Lemon, which was covered in 1850 as far as Sherborne Mill to reduce the stench off the water which took sewage from the houses and effluent from the brewery, and the leather and wool mills. The culvert is 13 feet wide and 8 feet high and is why there is such a hump in the roadway. The heavy rain in November 1894 coincided with a high tide and the river backed up in the culvert and overflowed into Harvey's corner

grocery, the Market House Inn, the Post Office, the Advertiser newspaper office, Rendell & Symons auctioneers, Webber's Coffee House, Norris's photographers, Hacker & Michelmore solicitors' office, the Sherborne Mill and the market pens holding bullocks and sheep. The residents may have preferred the fair's visit.

The Market Terrace houses still back onto the lower leat which can be seen behind the market's southern boundary wall. The leat's water drove the grinding wheels in Sherborne Corn Mill run by the Stockman family since 1838. In the road outside No 19 Market Street is a large manhole cover, made at Henry Beare's foundry in Salisbury Road, which marks the point where the mill leat joined the culverted river. The boundary between the parishes of Highweek and Wolborough ran along the leat and switched to the river at this point. Covering the river in 1850 had improved access to the market, but to enlarge the livestock market in 1904 Mr F. Zealley was contracted to culvert the rest of the river from Stockman's town mill to Hero Bridge.

The Passmore Edwards Public Library and the Science, Art and Technical School is now the Passmore Edwards Centre.

Market Street contains six listed buildings, but once contained more houses, shops and warehouses which have been demolished and replaced with other buildings or the urban park at Golden Lion Square. The Golden Lion Coaching House is the oldest remaining building.

Today the most impressive building in Market Street is the Science, Art and Technical School which dominates the corner site of Market Street and Highweek Street, but cannot be described without mention of its companion building in Highweek Street, the Passmore Edwards Public Library. They were combined into one in a multi-million pound refurbishment and extension project in 2012 and the Passmore Edwards Centre emerged. It is now run by a charity, Libraries Unlimited and amongst other things, houses the Railway Studies Collection. The edifice is a grade II listed building protected since 1983. The identity of each building is proclaimed in raised letter tiles spread around the two facades.

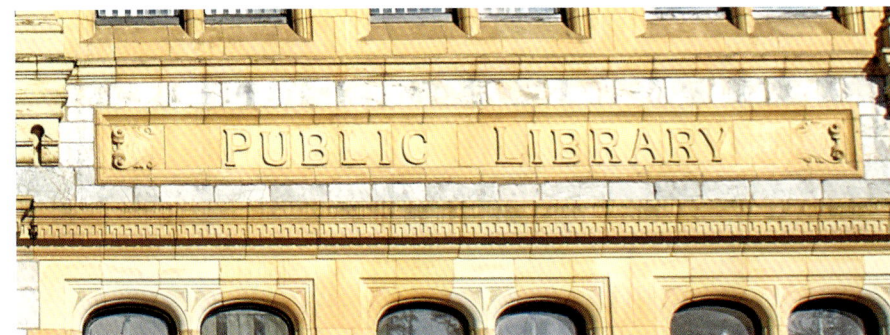

The Passmore Edwards Public Library had its entrance on Highweek Street and is a symmetrical building with two gables.

The Science, Art and Technical School is partly on Highweek Street and mainly on Market Street and is asymmetrical with six gables.

The L-shaped building wraps around a site once known as Harvey's Corner which was acquired and demolished by Devon County Council to widen the access road to the market and fortuitously was large enough to take the two conjoined buildings. Part of the left wing was the free library – a gift to Newton Abbot from the noted benefactor, John Passmore Edwards, in memory of his mother Susan who had been born in Wolborough Street near the Salem Chapel, now demolished. Passmore Edwards gave £2,290 to build the structure and a further £2,500 for fixtures, fittings and some books. The rest of the left wing and all the right wing was the Science, Art and Technical School, paid for by a grant from Devon County Council and public subscriptions. The building work was started by H. Goss of Torquay and when he failed, completed by F. A.A. Stacey of The Avenue, Newton Abbot.

Both parts of the three-storey building were designed by Cornish architect Silvanus Trevail in the flamboyant style he applied to all his designs. Started in 1901, this was Trevail's last commission as the architect committed suicide in 1903. His assistant, Alfred Cornelius completed the task in 1904.

The buildings are meant to be seen from the front and use ashlar blocks of Devon limestone and are richly detailed with yellow ceramic moulded dressings. There is a slate roof with ridge tiles pierced with a trefoil design and moulded chimney stacks. The rear and one side wall are in cream Hexter Humpherson brick laid in English bond (a row of long edges, a row of short ends); the remaining wall is of rough stone.

These highly decorative buildings have horizontal elements which work across both facades creating a visual harmony that closer inspection shows to be more complicated. At street level you will notice a plinth topped by moulded yellow blocks which runs around the two buildings, but sit in Golden Lion Square and you may spot the eleven – or is it twelve – other bands of ceramic detailing which cross your view. Likewise, the ground-

Ashlar or squared limestone and richly detailed yellow ceramic dressings

The basic window shape has four arched panes in two lights with a horizontal cross.

and first-floor windows appear to be all the same with four arched panes in two lights with a horizontal cross, but the spacing is not uniform, and on the second storey and the corner face there are all sorts of variations.

There is vertical continuity too, with the detailing becoming heavier as your eye scans upwards. All the first- and second-floor windows have pilasters dividing them. The second-floor windows have heavy rustication – large blocks alternating up the frame, with an apron of curved tiles below and a pediment above. The second floor has gables which rise above the gutter level, but of differing sizes. Marvellously there are neither gutters nor downpipes to spoil the facade.

It is the doorway of each building which sets them apart. The Passmore Edwards Public Library's central doorway on Highweek Street has a

The Passmore Edwards Public Library foundation stone

Rusticated pilasters flank the doorway

The dedication plaque reads 'This building was presented to the town by J. Passmore Edwards, Esq. in memory of his mother.'

A Renaissance style capital with two volutes, a central tulip head and a four-petalled flower.

foundation stone which sits at the bottom left and reads 'This stone was laid by the donor J. Passmore Edwards 9th October 1902. Charles Gilbert Vicary Esq. Chairman of the Public Library Committee.' Unfortunately, the last six words were lost from view when the pavement was raised. Having worked on the Committee since 1880, Charles Gilbert Vicary died in 1904, just before the building was opened. The library's imposing doorway has a solid deep-panelled double door in a flat dentilated arch, above which is the dedication plaque. There is a cornice over the top supported by two rusticated pilasters with wonderfully carved Renaissance style capitals, curled consoles and a triangular pediment which rise to the first floor.

There is a lot of other decoration on this relatively small building, but it has a more elaborate conjoined neighbour. To the same general design as the Passmore Edwards Public Library, Trevail has increased the density and complexity of the decorative elements on the Science, Art and Technical School building, with two different sized gables, a frieze of flowers, fruit and ribbon swags.

There is no gap between the Passmore Edwards Public Library and the Science, Art and Technical School building, but the junction is shown by an increase in height.

The Science, Art and Technical School doorway on the corner of Market Street and Highweek Street catches the eye at every storey. The Science, Art and Technical School foundation stone sits at the bottom left of the doorway, now the entrance to the Passmore Edwards Centre, and reads: 'This stone was laid by The Right Honourable Albert Edmund, 3rd Earl of Morley, Chairman of the Devon County Council, 9th October 1902. William Vicary, Esq., J.P. C.C. Chairman of Newton Abbot Urban District Council.' The stone was not big enough to get in Albert's surname, which was Parker, and directs you to the family seat at Saltram House. The 4th Earl inherited on Albert's death three years after he laid this stone and eventually Saltram was given to the National Trust.

The panelled double doors of this façade are under an elegant semicircular radial fanlight set in an arched doorcase with a Renaissance style surround. Termed a 'Gibbs doorway', the surround has heavily rusticated paired pilasters and a prominent segmental arch to form to the doorcase. Above this is a three-part decorative frieze with flowing shapes and an angelic face.

The first-floor three-light window

The Science, Art and Technical School's angel

sits between paired pilasters. The second-floor six-paned arched window is different to anything else on this building.

The original design by Trevail had a clock turret but this was too expensive and was replaced with a gable with more finials at the top. Under the ugly face of an abbot are the two shields of the towns which had amalgamated in 1901. Newton Bushel has barrels and Newton Abbot has a sheep, croziers, a mitre and the tower of Torre Abbey.

Rather than crane your neck at the two shields in the gable, step inside the doorway and inspect the same motif in the skilfully laid mosaic on the floor. The graceful art nouveau styling is of its time and doesn't borrow from the Renaissance or Jacobean.

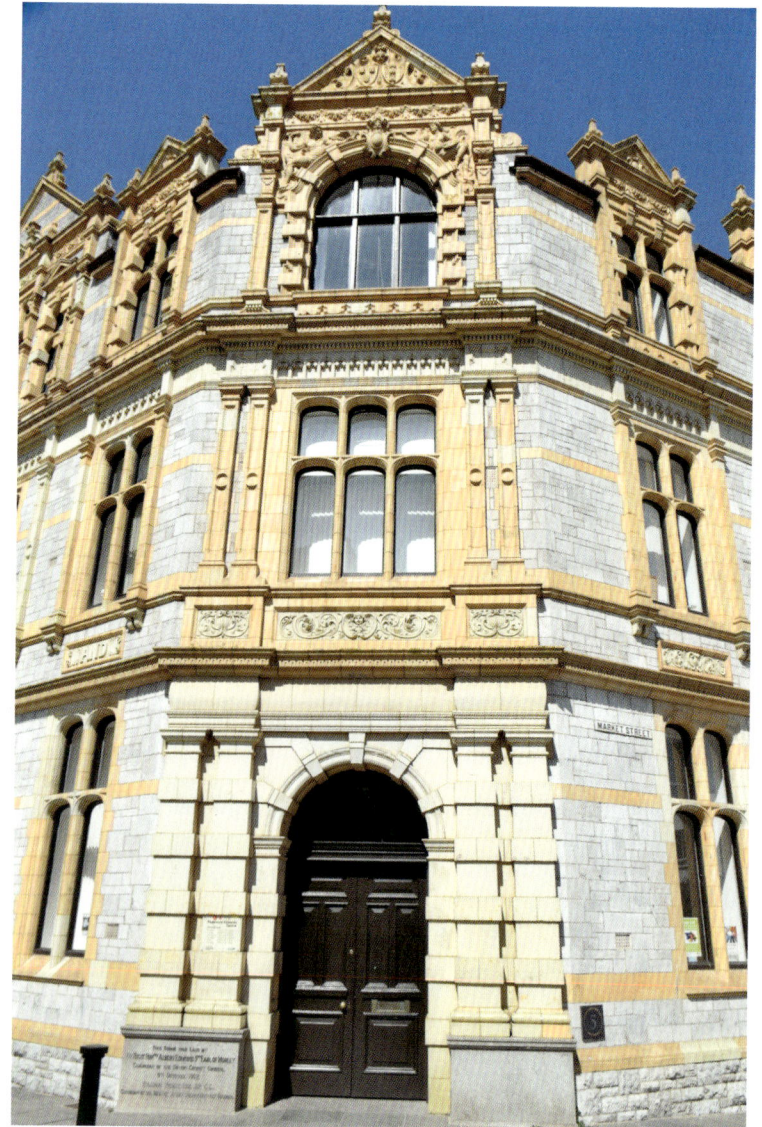

The impressive corner façade has little space for any more detailing.

The Science, Art and Technical School foundation stone

The pediment has two carved figures – he represents Science and she represents Art.

The two towns' shields Newton Bushel and Newton Abbot

The shields of Newton Bushel and Newton Abbot

Further inside, the two buildings reveal themselves again – not structurally, but in the detail. Go straight ahead and you are in the Science, Art and Technical School building. The staircase rises past the plain reed glass of the rear window and has a mahogany handrail sitting on turned bare balusters with a painted newel post and pendant at each turn. From the front door, go left into the old Passmore Edwards Public Library and cross the lobby with a patterned edge to the mosaic floor. The mahogany entrance doors lead to a Jacobean style unpainted mahogany staircase with newel posts, finials and pendants. This staircase rises past ornamental 'Literature' windows of leaded glass decorated with stylised pink and yellow flowers and the names of Homer, Milton and Shakespeare.

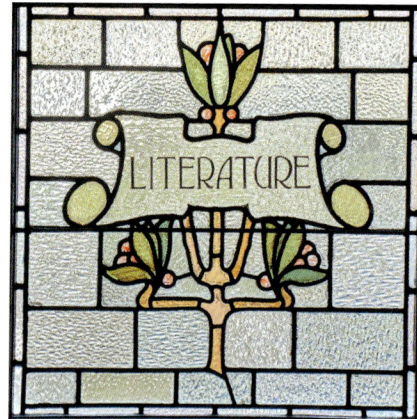

The Public Library had a three-bedroom flat on the second floor for the caretaker. In 1911 this was Frederick Chitty and his wife Esther. Frederick died in 1912 and Esther moved to Fisher Road. Both are buried in All Saints' graveyard, Highweek, and although Esther left £50 to the Church for the upkeep of their graves she is not mentioned in the burial records.

Richly decorated glass in the windows of the Library staircase

The original door joinery has some Art Nouveau brass handles.

An Ordnance Survey bench mark plate

The Science Art and Technical School building towers over No 1 and 3 Market Street.

Between the Passmore Edwards Centre and No 1 Market Street is an inconspicuous alleyway with a metal Ordnance Survey bench mark plate attached to the wall. It is the only one like it in the town.

The alley leads into the rear yard of the Market House, now known as the Market Gate. The licence for this had been held by William Harris for 13 years when it was transferred to James Madders, a poulterer by trade, in 1886. Unfortunately, he had periods when he was put into the County Mental Asylum in Exminster and Mrs Madders ran the pub, a rented cottage, a slaughter house and shop. When the Science, Art and Technical School was built next door, a bit of the Madders' land and their store was needed to create their access. The Madders insisted the store was taken down and rebuilt, and they were compensated for both loss of light, as the three-storey building towered above their yard, and loss of income as the scaffolding had made it impossible to let the cottage for two years.

An imposing 1913 building for a popular political party

No 7 Market Street was built as the Mid Devon Liberal Club in 1913/1914 and is a grade II listed building protected since 1983. The Mid Devon division had been Liberal since 1885 and hundreds attended when Charles Seale-Hayne, MP, opened their first club at No 1 Union Street in 1887. When it was announced that Ernest Morrison-Bell, a Conservative, had won the 1908 by-election it was the Liberal supporters who rioted in Union Street, but generally it was a social as well as political club. Members played whist, competed at billiards and rifle shooting, held lectures and dinners, raised money and went on outings. When the Union Street building proved too small for the membership, the Post Office on this Market Street site was purchased for £1,050 and demolished. It had been two houses in 1875 which the Post Office knocked into one and extended forwards to a new street line. Even so, this proved too small for the expanding postal trade, especially at Christmas when they had to take over the Alexandra Hall to sort over 7,000 parcels. The Post Office moved to Bank Street and this three-storey club was designed by Josias Crocker

Beare (1881-1962), the youngest son of Henry Beare, a local foundry family. Those who describe the design style of this 1913 building differ in opinion. You can choose – is it Edwardian Baroque, or Italian Renaissance of the Florentine or Venetian School? Whatever your view, Beare's design has a distinguished façade with painted stucco walls incised to look like stone with quoins running up the outer edges. The symmetry of the building was compromised by the need for a separate office which was tucked into the right hand of the ground floor. It has a small door and a tripartite window. The higher status club entrance has wide double doors under a three-pane overlight with a deep cornice held up by two elaborately carved consoles, and the name of the establishment is writ large.

The upper two floors do display perfect symmetry. They are separated by a moulded string course which widens to provide a step below the central loggia and a cornice above the two outer windows of the first floor. Each cornice shelters a cartouche with a scroll frieze. Compare this with the similar shape of cartouche on the corner of the Passmore Edwards Centre.

The covered exterior gallery or loggia is unique in the town and has three arches which spring off six Ionic columns, flanked by two square pilasters. The top of each arch has a dropped keystone. At the front are three stone balustrades (one replaced baluster is a different shape) and behind are three French windows giving access to the loggia, maybe intended for announcements of election success. The second floor was the caretaker's apartments, occupied by Mr and Mrs Ryder in 1915. This floor has four plate-glass sash windows with moulded frames and flat brackets under the sill. To finish off the building, there is a moulded egg and dart frieze below the closely spaced eave dentils.

The central foundation stone reads: 'This stone was laid by Lady Bowring of London 29th November 1913. Herbert Holman Esq. J. P. President. Robert Vicary esq. J.P. C.C. Chairman'. A prominent Liberal, Lady Bowring was accompanied on the day by her husband Sir Thomas, and although the stone refers to their London address, they were better known for their Moretonhampstead connections, where they had funded social housing. Perhaps this place name was too long for the stone? Herbert Holman was the Liberal candidate for the local constituency and President of the local Liberals with Robert Vicary as Chairman.

The architect, Josias Crocker Beare, enlisted in the First World War and was a Second Lieutenant in the Hampshire (Fortress) Royal Engineers in 1915, but he was back in Newton Abbot in 1919 to eventually design 32 houses built at Milber and the unique Meter Testing building in Quay Road.

The Mid Devon Liberal Club foundation stone

The egg and dart moulding under the eave dentils

Compare this cartouche on the Liberal Club and that on the library

No 9 and 11 Market Street are grade II listed buildings protected since 1996. They were built in the mid-1800s as three-storey houses but are now offices. They are stepped back from the road edge as they once had gardens in front with a path to each door. The doorways sit on the left-hand side of each house in a moulded arch with a six-panelled door under a semicircular fanlight. Each house has five windows in moulded architraves. The ground floor windows are 8/8 pane sash windows, the second floor has plate glass sash windows and the third floor has 4/8 sashes. A wide eave has widely spaced dentils.

Although not a listed building, No 13 Market Street has some interesting styling. The red brick plinth has four pilasters which rise to the string course between the two storeys. The two outer edge, giant-order pilasters then rise to a wide eave. Above the two square ground-floor windows and the central six-panel door, are matching tall brick arches with a cream keystone that hold a fanlight. The arches are linked across the frontage by hood mouldings, broken by the pilasters. The two boot scrapers show it was built when the roads were not paved. It now houses Rendells, formerly Rendell and Symons, established in 1816.

Sixteen windows and four doors of Wollens offices

Next door to Rendells is a row of plain buildings, now Wollens offices. No 15, 17 and 19 were built as three houses with three 6/6 sash windows each with moulded surrounds, although some have lost the brackets under the sill. Each house has a tall door to the left, two with boot scrapers. The entrance is at No 19 and has two steps up to the lobby, fluted door jambs with two simple consoles supporting a plain cornice overhead. The double door has a 1930s style overlight with strong horizontal framing. No 21 has seven 6/6 sash windows and a door to the right.

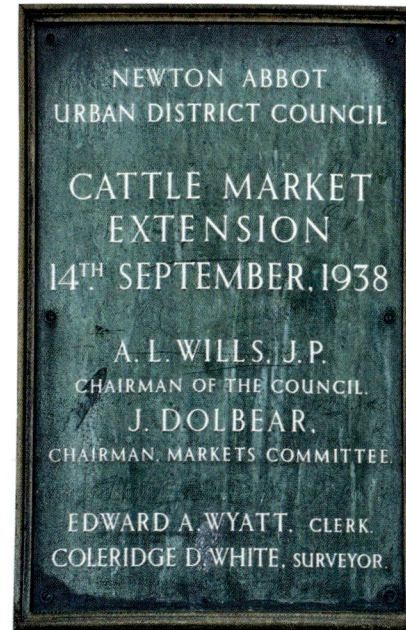

The last building on this side of the road is obscured by a functional bus shelter, but the informative inscription says it all. It is the 1938 offices for the market staff and auctioneers built by Newton Abbot Urban District Council. The sinuous façade has a plinth, and eleven pilasters capped by square capitals joined by a parapet. Six original windows have eight square pane overlights. The remaining windows and doors have been amended. Negotiations for the market extension started in 1930 as the existing areas for livestock had become congested with the increased trade. A tally in 1934 recorded 34,500 animals brought to market and this trebled over the following four years. As the prosperity of the town was dependent on the market trade, it was decided to purchase and demolish Sherborne Mill, half of the houses in Mill Lane/Halcyon Road, Minerva House's gardens and the Commercial Inn to release the land for a cattle market extension. The public right of way across the cattle market extension shows the route of the road alongside the mill joining Market Street to Mill Lane, now called Halcyon Road.

The plans received the Ministry of Health's approval and £40,000 was borrowed and raised for the works. Tenders for drainage, roads and steelwork went out in 1937 to build the loading pens, covered pens and ring for animal sales, secure bull pens and rows of tie-rings for each cow and her calf. The changes made Newton Abbot market the second largest facility in Devon.

A date stone to celebrate the year the building was finished

The Alexandra Cinema, once a theatre, once a corn exchange, always looks like an Italian church

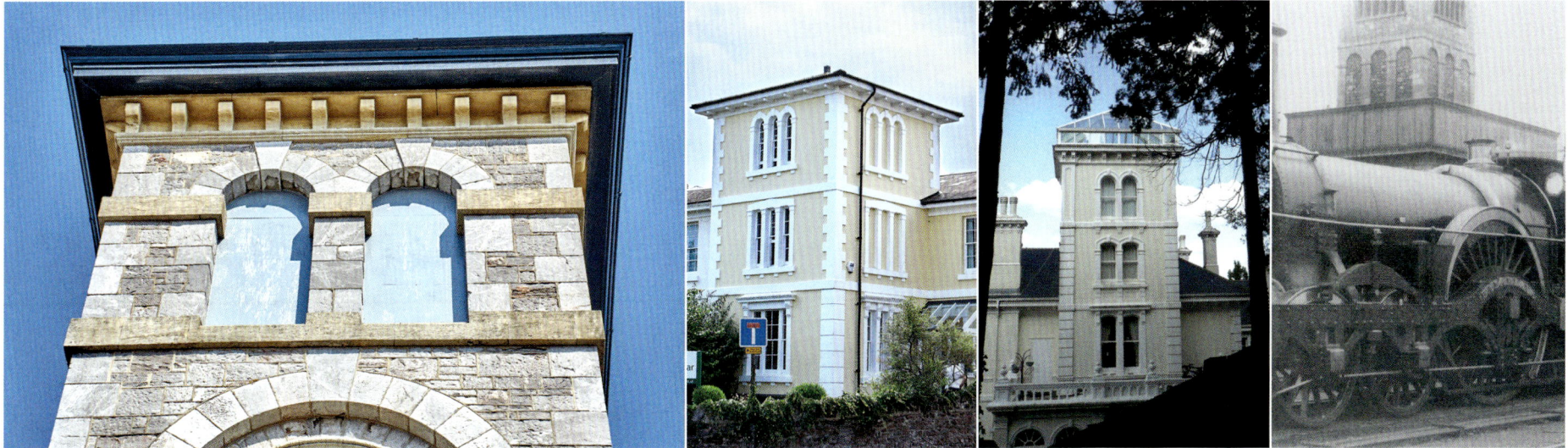

Comparing towers. Left to right: Alexandra Cinema, Tower House, Highwood and Newton Abbot's pumping station

The Alexandra Cinema is a grade II listed building, protected since 1972, and built as a corn exchange. It was designed by John Chudleigh junior, of Newton Abbot, and built by J. Harvey and Sons of Torquay for £6,000. The Devon limestone walls have some Bath stone detailing and some painted stucco. The three-stage, 57-foot tower has an impressive, semicircular entrance doorway with voussoirs that stand out, leading to a dropped keystone at the top. Above this is a square panel with a stone which reads 'Erected 1871'.

This stone is separated from the storey above by closely space dentils under a wide sill band. On top of this is an arch containing a circular window, shielded by a hood mould with carved leaf stops. The third storey has a pair of arched windows on each face with wide eaves under a shallow-pitched pyramidal roof. Coupled with the five semicircular arched windows each side of the auditorium, the whole has the look of an Italian church. The top of the tower can be compared with the Tower House in Courtenay Park,

Highwood House and Newton Abbot's atmospheric pumping station. Three rare images of the latter, demolished in 1897, can be found in the museum archives in Newton's Place, Wolborough Street.

As you would expect of a cinema, few windows of the Alexandra have glass. A functional fire exit indicates the time when the upper floor second screen was added in 1996. The two semicircular additions either side of the tower entrance are where farmers once paid their market tolls.

Inside there was a 60- x 40-foot

hall with a fine beamed roof with iron spandrels. The hot air and tobacco smoke left through two ventilators in the roof. Here the traders were supposed to transact their business, but they had always done their deals in the street and continued to do so after this building had been erected. The Corn Exchange became the Alexandra Hall in 1874 and was subsequently used for all sorts of entertainments, dinners, meetings, exhibitions and auctions until it became a theatre with a screen, then a cinema with a stage.

The companion to the Alexandra Cinema is the pannier market hall attached to the rear. It was built in the same style for the sale of anything other than a live animal. Several entrances lead into a space 161 feet long and 77 feet wide. The 30-foot high cast-iron columns branch out into 'bubbles' of metal and lead up to a continuous clerestory window, and then seemingly thin wrought iron holds up the roof. There are six shops on one side, divided by seven substantial granite pillars. The remaining space is filled with stalls which sell a wide range of goods.

Substantial granite columns divide the six shops.

Newton Abbot Pannier Market

Teignbridge District Council
in partnership with SWH Build

The 'bubble' spandrels have become a motif for the pannier market.

Next to the Alexandra Cinema is the Jolly Farmer, once called the Bradley Hotel. It had been an inn since before 1829 and was part of the Reverend Richard Lane's Bradley estates. The first floor render has been removed revealing the random rubble walls, but the detailing around the windows and doors has been retained.

At the beginning of Market Street, stand in front of the Passmore Edwards Public Library, and you will see the generosity of one man, but the three foundation stones in Market Street show the work of an entire family. The three brothers, William, Robert and Charles Vicary, were sons of John Vicary. Look towards Bradley Lane and you would have seen the J. Vicary & Sons leather tanning yards, now demolished, and beyond are the former J. Vicary & Sons woollen mills. The Vicary family would have employed thousands of men since they arrived in Highweek in the mid-1740s. They supported and represented the interests of their employees, made sure they had the opportunity to advance themselves through reading, schooling and – to their minds – Liberal politics. William Vicary was the first Chairman of the new Urban District Council when Newton Abbot and Newton Bushel were combined in 1901.

The fourth inscription has the names, positions and roles of just four of the men of Newton Abbot Urban District Council who guided and decided the plans for the market extension. The last named, Coleridge D. White, joined the Urban District Council as Surveyor in 1908 and his conscientious work over the next 31 years shaped much of the town we see today.

The building on the corner of Golden Lion Square has fabulous corner windows.

Sherborne Road

Sherborne Road only has modern buildings today, but it was once the site of Newton Bushel's Sherborne Mill, first documented as 'Scirborne Mill' in 1324 and as 'Seyrborne Mills' in 1407. It was referred to as 'Newton Mills' in 1832 and often called Stockman Mills after that family bought it in 1838. It had four wheels milling wheat to produce flour, driven by a constant supply of water through leats off the River Lemon near Bradley Manor. It was purchased and demolished by Newton Abbot Urban District Council for the market extension of 1938 as were a row of twelve cottages called Fern Terrace. The most remarkable building remaining is the multi-storey car park which is an abstract artist's delight.

On the outside wall of the market's sheep pens is a panel of tiles entitled Dartmoor Landscape by Yasuharu Tajima-Simpson (Taja) placed here in 1996. Taja also devised the roundels in Courtenay Street.

Dartmoor Landscape, by Taja

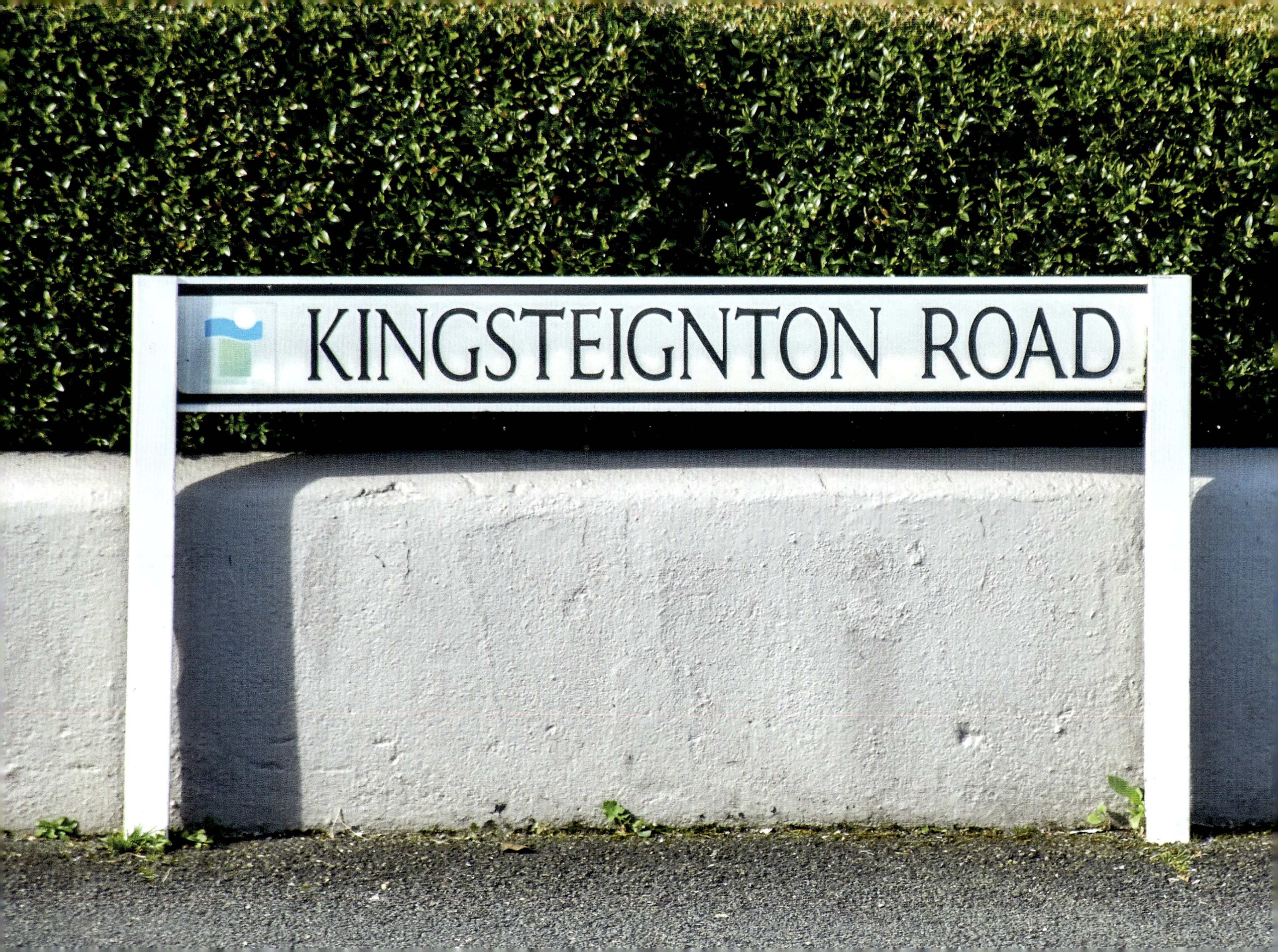
KINGSTEIGNTON ROAD

Kingsteignton Road starts halfway across Hero Bridge as the parish boundary runs down the centre of the River Lemon, which emerges from the culvert below. The road crosses the Whitelake Channel Bridge and ends just beyond the Kingsteignton Road Bridge over the railway line to Moretonhampstead, built in 1864 where, surprisingly, it does not meet Kingsteignton but Teigngrace parish. This parish's boundary is so convoluted it must follow ancient drainage ditches, river courses and land ownerships no longer visible in the landscape. Perhaps James Templar of Stover had a hand in it to ensure the Stover Canal lies wholly in this parish.

There are no listed buildings in Kingsteignton Road.

Hero Bridge and Kingsteignton Road were built in 1842. Hero Cottages existed nearby in 1851 and the bridge was mentioned in 1854 as the highest tidal point on the River Lemon. In 1882 Hero Bridge became a County Bridge and one stone in the wall under the massive Dartmoor granite capping stones would have been engraved with a 'C' to show the County Council workers which bridges they maintained. It may still be there below street level.

When it really was a bridge, Hero Bridge was the location of a May Day tradition, thankfully no longer practiced. The boys from Highweek parish would gather on the Kingsteignton Road side of the bridge and the Wolborough parish boys would gather on the Courtenay Street side and they would throw stones at each other until one group retreated – just for fun.

Hero Bridge had its name before 1854

The design of Sherborne House is in keeping with the town, but the size is not.

The imposing modern office building, Sherborne House, has a four-storey steel frame with walls of red brick with cream brick detailing, and three entrance façades of rendered panels. The roof is of man-made slates. It was commissioned by the Department of the Environment and built by Midas Construction for the Inland Revenue. It was officially opened in 1993 by the Director General, Clive Corlett, and is no longer used by this government office.

At one time the next interesting building in Kingsteignton Road was the Newton Abbot Rural District Council Offices. They once had offices in the Union Workhouse in East Street, but when they had a chance to build a new office in 1936, they chose a site in Kingsteignton Road and built a beautiful two-storey building, suitably low to comply with the ruling on the height and not obscuring the view of the houses on Knowles Hill. It cost £6,400 to build and was opened by Mrs Whiteway-Wilkinson, wife of the Chairman in January 1937. The frontage was symmetrical in five shallow bays divided by major and minor pilasters with triangular capitals. The two outer bays contained a large square window on each storey, the two inner bays had three smaller windows with a fluted panel separating the storeys. The central bay had an impressive entrance sitting under a geometric Moderne styled window. It had 14

A once beautiful building, last occupied by Devon County Council, now replaced with homes.

offices and a council chamber to seat 50 members. The detailing inside was stylish with wood panelling, curving, yet square, brass handrails to the sweeping staircase, terrazzo flooring and coffered ceilings.

When it opened, the Council officers dealt with the business of nearly thirty parishes with a population of over twenty thousand people. With local government reorganisation in 1974 it became the Chief Executive's department of Teignbridge District Council and was kept in immaculate order. In a bid to cut costs new offices were built next to Forde House so that all satellite offices became centralised. This building became part of Devon County Council's property holdings, used by Social Services and allowed to deteriorate until it was demolished in 2014.

The curving, yet square rails to Teignbridge District Council's Chief Executive's Department offices

The long-gone letter box to the 1936 building

The Mill was once the Devon Leathercrafts factory

The building now occupied by The Mill was built in 1930 as a factory for Devon Leathercrafts which manufactured and hand finished small leather goods. The business was started by ex-Royal Irish Constabulary officer Louis Harold Carter in 1922. He filed a patent in 1929 for an 'initial letter button cover' to personalise a wallet or purse which proved highly successful. He showed this and other products at the British Industries Fairs in the early 1930s and travelled to the USA to expand the business. Carter died in 1957 and the business declined in the face of foreign competition until it ceased trading in 1984. The building was used as a pottery, then left empty until renovated and revamped from a dull three-storey square factory into the four-storey building containing offices and flats. The added top floor has arched and triangular pediments over the windows and the lower storey square windows have had a string course added to divide each floor level.

Behind The Mill are the remains of John Vicary's Bark Mill, leased from the Duke of Somerset and used to mash tree bark to release the tannins used in leather processing.

News from the Bark Mill was mostly bad. Between 1844 and 1874 the newspapers report people being caught in the grinding wheels and falling off ricks of bark with the inevitable loss of limb and life. As the use of locally sourced bark dried up, Teignmouth's shipping reports show the Vicarys importing valonia oak bark from Greece in 1902 for use in the tanning process.

Kings Mews is a private house at the junction of Kingsteignton Road and Jetty Marsh Road, next to the steps which climb 45 feet to the viewpoint over the eastern side of the town, sometimes called Breakneck Hill.

Fittingly, Kings Mews was a horseshoe-shaped set of stables with a house, all constructed from limestone with red brick detailing around the windows, ventilation grilles, and doors. From the two imposing gateposts can be seen the large yard, paved with Hexter Humpherson brick, and a two-storey row of stables which had hay lofts, a harness room and duty room for two grooms, now used for furniture removals. There was once a second row of stabling. At the head of the yard is a two-storey, five-roomed house.

From 1879 until his disappearance in 1893 it was occupied by Hugh Barratt. He ran a livery stable here hiring out and selling horses and carriages. He often won prizes for his mares and hunters at the Devon County Show and West of England Horse Show. Hugh's father was a colt and pony breaker, trainer and dealer at Puddaven, near Totnes. Hugh took on this business when his father died in 1883 and over the next seven years held sales at both sites using jockeys to move horses between his properties, customers and grazing.

By 1891 Kings Mews house was rented and Hugh lived at 12, Lower St Paul's Road, now known as The Avenue. A notice in the papers in December 1893 stated Barratt couldn't pay the rent and had to sell horses, wagons and harness sets. Then bankruptcy papers were served against him but he was nowhere to be found. A month later his possessions were seized and sold to repay his debts and the mews was let. Fred Bulley, a horse trainer from Hopkins Mews, and married to Hugh's sister, took on the building and Barrett's business. Dogged by a series of mishaps to himself and the death of one of his jockeys, Fred gave up in 1898. H.W. Thomas of Hele House, Highweek took on Kings Mews selling horses to the Government. On one day in 1899, 36 horses of all grades were loaded onto trains at Newton Abbot station and shipped to the South African War. Thomas was followed by Sellwood, then Davies selling horses until 1933 by which time it was used as a dairy farm with cows grazing on the Jetty Marshes. Fred Bulley died in 1939 aged 80, described as a fearless jockey, trainer, horse dealer and coachman, but the location of Hugh Barratt remains a mystery.

Hundreds of horses would have been sold at Kings Mews.

Wolborough Street

Wolborough Street is an ancient route, later a turnpike, from Newton Abbot to Totnes. It was once called High Street and starts at the junction with East Street, Courtenay Street and Bank Street and ends at the beginning of Totnes Road, with several roads and courts of houses off to the left and right.

St Leonard's Chapel Tower west-facing side

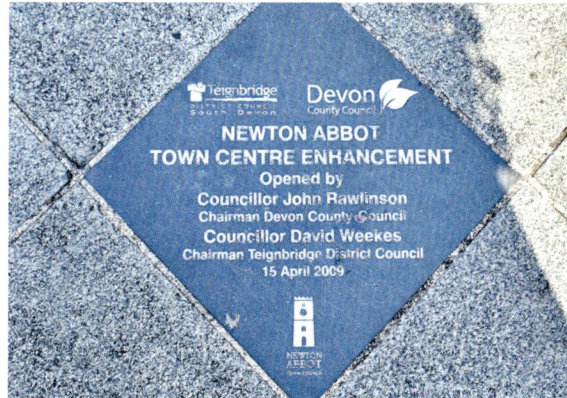

Pedestrianisation of the area around St Leonard's Chapel and naming it Besigheim Place, to acknowledge the town's twin town in Germany, was completed in 2009.

There are 28 listed buildings in Wolborough Street, but there are others of note.

The most obvious building at the start of Wolborough Street is St. Leonard's Chapel Tower. It is one of only two grade II* listed buildings in Newton Abbot and has been protected since 1949, but not before, as the tower is all that remains, above ground, of a 13th century chapel of rest for the parish of Wolborough. The nave of the chapel was demolished in 1836 to widen the road under powers given to the Totnes Bridgetown Pomeroy Turnpike Trust in 1824 'to take down and remove certain Market Houses, Buildings, and Obstructions in the Towns of Newton Abbot.' Ironically the tower is now in a pedestrianised area.

The interesting railings in Besigheim Place were designed by Peter Osborne.

The tower is built mainly of squared local limestone, some flattened, some rough, but you can also spot bits of mottled grey granite, black spillite and red sandstone in the walls. The stonework has been given a raised mortar finish, creating some visual uniformity. It has three stages, divided by a string course of thin slabs of stone between the lower and upper floors, and between the upper floor and the crenelated parapet.

The west-facing side has the entrance, with a pointed arch which is worth closer scrutiny as it is composed of two fine pieces of carved granite at the top, but below these are mismatched granite pieces, carved later with a single edging groove. The piece at the bottom right-hand side has the stone-cutter's signature of two lines, like an upside-down letter T.

Set in the arch is a relatively modern studded plank door with a twisted metal handle above a plain lock plate. The key is solid, long-shafted and weighty.

To the upper right of the door is a small oblong window which sheds some light on the staircase inside. There is another one on the north

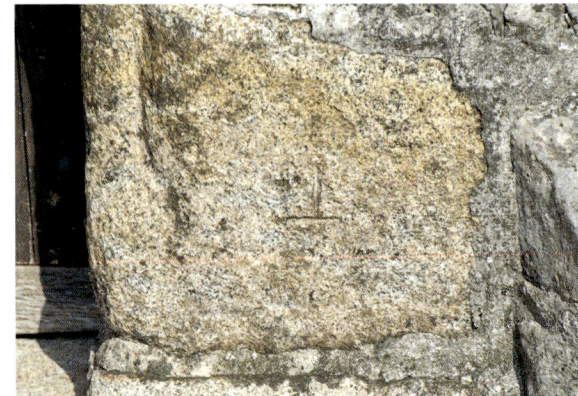

The stone-cutter's mark — he would have been paid per piece made.

Odd and mismatched stones have been used around the chapel door.

face. These are only slightly larger than the tiny window in Pound Place, off Wolborough Street. Above the door is a pointed-arched window with two lights divided by a carved stone mullion. There are large clock faces on the west- and east-facing walls, and each side of the tower has a pair of louvred lancet windows to the bell chamber.

The corner between the west- and north-facing sides holds a block of red sandstone incised with the arrow and line of an Ordnance Survey bench mark. Surveyors used these marks to plan buildings and lay pipes. The line here was known to be 23.7 feet above sea level, but is no longer maintained as the Ordnance Survey now uses GPS (Global Positioning System).

The east-facing side shows the roof line of the demolished nave and has a single, trefoil-topped window set in the old archway. Stretching out from this face, the extent of the chapel is shown by small black square tiles carved with the symbols of the Abbots of Torre, the one-time owners of Newton Abbot.

The two inscribed plaques on the tower add to the history of this building, commemorating Councillor

Abbot of Torre's symbols are cut into tiles to mark the extent of the nave.

The Ordnance Survey bench mark cut into sandstone is now obsolete.

A carronade made in Scotland, taken by the Chinese, and recaptured by the British

The Wolborough market cross base was reused to commemorate William of Orange's arrival in England.

Arthur Claude Shobbrook on one side and Queen Victoria on the other.

At the foot of the tower is a well-rubbed stone which was placed here to deflect traffic before it hit the wall. The roadway on this side was narrow and took all of the cart and cattle traffic on market day, but the other side was wider as it was where the market stalls were set up.

Unusually, the two small carronades on the nave side were listed in 1983 as grade II. They were made at the Carron Foundry in Falkirk, Scotland, for British merchant ships. The story goes that they were taken by Chinese pirates, but the Royal

Navy 'repatriated' them in an action against the pirates in the Yangtse River in 1874 and they were given to Newton Abbot in about 1901 when Newton Abbot and Newton Bushel became one town.

Also on this side of the tower is the base of the old Wolborough market cross, thought to date from the 1600s, and is a grade II listed structure. It is built with carved granite blocks which make an octagon with a barrel shape above and the shallow, bevelled cap supports a lamp. The barrel was later carved with an inscription which reads 'The First Declaration of William III, Prince of Orange, the Glorious

Defender of the Protestant Religion and the Liberties of England, was read on this pedestal by the Rev John Reynel, Rector of this Parish on the 5th November 1688.' Now set in stone are two errors. The Prince arrived in Brixham on 5 November 1688 and took two days to get to Newton Abbot, so the declaration was read on the 7th, and the Reverend's surname is properly spelled Reynell. The lettering, with its errors, was renewed by the Reverend William Langley Pope in 1887 to commemorate Queen Victoria's Jubilee.

Few interesting features remain on No 2 Wolborough Street.

The monogrammed doorway mosaic for Frank Halsé & Co in No 2 Wolborough Street

No 2 Wolborough Street, which curves around the corner into Bank Street, was once a grander building. The ground floor retains its three plate-glass windows with the many small panes above and its sheltering doorway, but on the two storeys above all decoration has been erased. It once had four pilasters dividing three sets of 6/6 sash windows with fine pediments to the first floor and moulded architraves to the second floor. The building was topped by two stone balustrades either side of a low wall.

The best retained feature is Frank Halsé's mosaic monogram set in the doorway floor. His story is a sad tale to tell. He had separated from his wife Gertrude in 1919. They had two children and Frank sent regular cheques to support them. When the youngest was nine years old, Frank exercised his agreed right to have the two children for the summer and sent extra money to cover the costs. Ready to leave for the station, a policeman arrived at Frank's door. His three children had been hanged by his wife, then she had hanged herself. Frank thought that he had misheard the number of children, but at the inquest he discovered that his wife had a third child and had told her neighbours that her husband had drowned. Knowing her children would talk about their sister to Frank and talk about Frank to her neighbours, she felt compelled to end it all. Frank continued to live and work in Newton Abbot until his death in 1935.

No 1 to 3 Wolborough Street have gables facing the street, which indicates early buildings.

No 1 and 3 Wolborough Street are grade II listed buildings, protected since 1949. They were built in the 1600s as three two-storey houses and are timber-framed. The walls are of painted render rising to three gables which face the street. There are two chimney stacks which were raised in height with cream bricks some time in the 1800s when taller houses were built next door and impeded the air flow.

No 1 is on the corner of East Street and is shown as a Court House in 1843. The ground floor has an early 1900s shop front with plate-glass windows with leaded top windows. On the first floor there is a six-light mullion window set back from the ground floor, and some rusticated quoins can be seen on the right-hand side of the front wall. The second house has a recessed window with four lights on the ground floor. The third house, No 3, has a late 1800s shop front with decorative upper corners. On the first floor of the middle and right houses are two 1900s eight-light oriel windows, which jut out on short brackets. These two gables each have a small square window. No 3's gable has the vestiges of slate-hanging, now heavily painted.

No 1 Wolborough Street was the Court House.

The overlapping slates hung high in the eaves of No 3 kept the timber frame dry.

Between the second and third houses is a rare survivor – a doorway with a much-beaten 1600s panelled and studded plank door with a wrought-iron strap hinge ending in a fleur-de-lys tip.

No 5 and 7 Wolborough Street are grade II and protected since 1983. They are symmetrical 1600s, three-storey houses of painted render which were re-fronted to create two shops with flats above, with three modern windows on each floor. No 7 has an interesting collection of 1930s glass in the rear half of the shop.

No 5 and 7 Wolborough Street were re-fronted after the 1600s.

The interesting inter-war Moderne glass in No 7 is almost as good as in the Passmore Edwards Centre.

Between the shops is a doorway which has white-lettered, blue tiles above, stating it is No 1 Court, once known as Branscombe's Court. Behind the door is a passageway with walls protected by horizontal planking which once led to 11 small hovel cottages. They were being built behind the shop by bakers Elizabeth and Charlotte Branscombe when the census was taken in 1851. This same year there were 17 other courts off the length of Wolborough Street with 130 small dwellings occupied by 490 people.

No 9 Wolborough Street was once the Ship Inn. It is a grade II listed building, protected since 1983. It is a two-storey, mid-1600s building of painted pebble dash over a timber frame. It was re-fronted to change the first-floor windows and create a shop front, now a restaurant.

Almost lost from view are the blue and white tiles naming this No 1 Court.

No 9 Wolborough Street was once the Ship, a reminder of the town's maritime past.

No 11 Wolborough Street is a grade II listed building protected since 1983. It is a 1600s or earlier two-storey inn once known as The Bear. It is of painted stucco probably over a timber frame. The ground floor now has shop fronts. The first floor has two windows with late 1800s paired plate-glass horned sash windows. The 'horn' hangs under the top frame and strengthens the joint. It also saves your fingers if the sash cord breaks and the top window falls. The central semi-elliptical arch is over a very wide 1800s panelled door leading to a through-passage. All public houses near the market had a slaughterhouse at the back where you could have your recent purchase butchered or you could buy your meat for the week.

The through-passage under a shallow arch of No 11 Wolborough Street led to a slaughterhouse.

The new Armoury replaced the old Armoury in East Street, demolished to extend Marks & Spencer's shop.

The red brick building now occupied by Austin's Toy Department was once the Armoury. It was built for the Devonshire Territorial Association in April 1913 for the use of E Company, 5th (Prince of Wales) Devon Regiment of the Territorial Force. The building was officially opened by Colonel F. G. L. Lamotte, Commander of the Devon and Cornwall Infantry Brigade and included a cream brick gymnasium and drill hall to the rear, still to be seen from the first-floor windows. The three sash windows at the front of the first floor have orange brick aprons beneath them and are flanked by two plain pilasters topped by stylised shields in orange brick beneath a capping stone. An eave band and cornice are supported by dentilations.

At street level there were once four low-silled windows and a double door with two semicircular windows. The very open-to-view front was to encourage young men to peek in, be captivated by the Army lifestyle and join up. Under Captain Gilbert Doke Vicary in 1913 were 140 non-commissioned Officers (NCOs) and men, and six officers. Although a partner in the Vicary Woollen Mills, G. D. Vicary enlisted and died of wounds received in Palestine on 8 November 1917. His ten family members were joined by hundreds of mourners at his memorial service at St Mary's Church, Abbotsbury. Brigadier General Frank Grimshaw Lagier Lamotte survived service in both the South African and First World Wars and died in 1938.

No 13 Wolborough Street was re-fronted in inter-war Moderne style, but at the back was once a private garden.

Carpetright is on the corner of Wolborough Street and Newfoundland Way and was designed by architects of the Ratcliffe Groves Partnership of Bury, London and Glasgow, which also designs houses, offices and factories. The ground floor retail unit has apartments on two storeys above and it may never become a listed building.

Newfoundland Way

Newfoundland Way is a relatively new road built to bypass the busy junction around St Leonard's Chapel Tower. It was named after the cod fishing area off east-coast Canada where local families ventured from the 1700s onwards. When built it truncated or demolished the sites of No 1 Court to No 5 Court as well as gardens, yards and storage in Wolborough Street. Other courts off Wolborough Street and other parts of the town were demolished without record earlier in the 1900s. However, between 1983 and 1985 several properties were surveyed before demolition and evidence at nearby No 34–46 Wolborough Street revealed that there had been buildings there since the 1200s, with major changes in each subsequent century as houses and small industrial sites were rearranged, subdivided or replaced. Substantial rebuilding in the 1800s created shops with archways to give access to the rear courts.

The open roadways and car parks viewed from Newfoundland Way may make you believe Wolborough Street has ended but it continues westwards from St. Leonard's Church, now called Newton's Place.

The former Church of St Leonard, Wolborough Street, is a grade II listed building, protected since 1983. It was built with Devon limestone rubble under a slate roof in 1835 by Richard Millward to replace St Leonard's Chapel of Ease in Wolborough Street, the nave of which was demolished for road widening. A chancel was added and interior alterations made in 1876 by Joseph W. Rowell. The church was converted into a community space, museum and offices for Newton Abbot Town Council in 2020.

The front is symmetrical in three bays. At ground level the left and right bays once had granite steps leading to a door in pointed arches under simple hood moulding which shed the water away from the people below. Above them are matching two-light traceried windows and the walls end in sloped gables which spread their weight onto stone kneelers. The central bay is stepped forward and flanked by two octagonal turrets topped with crenelated crown-like parapets. At street level the remains of the iron railings can be seen in the granite floor slabs leading to a wide flight of four granite steps, flanked by cast-iron boot scrapers. The two doorways sit in pointed arches with five lobed windows. Over the arches are hood mouldings with decorative ends. On the first storey a large four-light traceried window with three multi-lobed windows sits in a pointed arch. The glass of this window is best

Earl of Devon's coronet, gold shield, blue lions and three red torteaux. The Latin motto Quod Verum Tutum means What is True is Right.

Newton's Place: The town's museum occupies part of the former St Leonard's Church.

One of the nine diamond-paned, tall, pointed, three-light windows under hood mouldings. The tenth has no glass.

seen from inside as it has the crest of the Earl of Devon who owned much of Wolborough and Newton Abbot and gave the land and money to build the church.

There are lancet recesses in the apex; the tallest is louvred for the bell.

Along either side of the chancel are leaded diamond-paned windows under hood moulding. The first window in the left-hand wall of the chancel has always been blocked as it was built against an existing building, since demolished. The Ordnance Survey bench mark on the right-hand corner of the building was known to be 26.3 feet above sea level.

The 1876 vestry and chancel extension at the rear is built of squared limestone on two storeys. At ground level there are two arched windows with hood mouldings holding stained-glass windows. Beyond these windows there are three granite steps which lead to a planked door with elaborate strap hinges and a further three steps leads to a shouldered-arched doorway typical of Rowell's designs. This single-storey lean-to has three windows with diamond-leaded plain glass. The upper clerestory has three shallow arches on each side holding three-light windows and the impressive East Window has wonderful scenes from the life of Jesus dedicated to Thomas Mackrell and Thomas Hatch. All the coloured glass is by Francis Drake and best viewed from inside the museum.

The gallery above the museum has been converted into meeting spaces and is 'supported' by slender cast-iron columns with faces of men and animals as capitals, as well as substantial modern steelwork. The shallow-pitched nave ceiling has foliate bosses. The floor of the chancel has polychromatic tiles and the walls have pointed stone arches resting on paired colonettes supported by corbels. None of the stonework designs are repeated. The octagonal stone pulpit has five recesses with statues of three French saints, a king and a bishop. The chancel has a richly painted panelled ceiling with flowers and angels. There is an anachronism – a 15th century octagonal font sits in this Victorian church. It was the gift of the Earl of Devon and was originally in Salcombe Church.

The vestry and chancel extension of 1876

St Leonard's Road

St Leonard's Road, once Terrace, is named after the church on the corner and has a mixture of buildings, in style and size, built between 1863 and modern times. Of the five handsome double-fronted houses that bend around St Leonard's to Jubilee Road, No 64 is noteworthy as it was once a 'scattered home'. This was part of a system of foster homes in Newton Abbot where children from the workhouse were placed with a fostering adult who would ensure they went to school and church, and ultimately into apprenticeships, the forces or service rather than back into the Union Workhouse in East Street. Beatrice Stabb was promoted from an assistant in a scattered home in Highweek to being in charge in this home in 1912. Aged 21, she was paid £22 a year to look after 11 boys.

The houses all have a plinth and plat band, four of the five houses have four 6/6 hornless sash windows and a blind central first-floor window. One house has a fifth window and incised stucco in a stone block pattern. Each door is recessed under an elegant arch with simple pilasters, a keystone and an overlight.

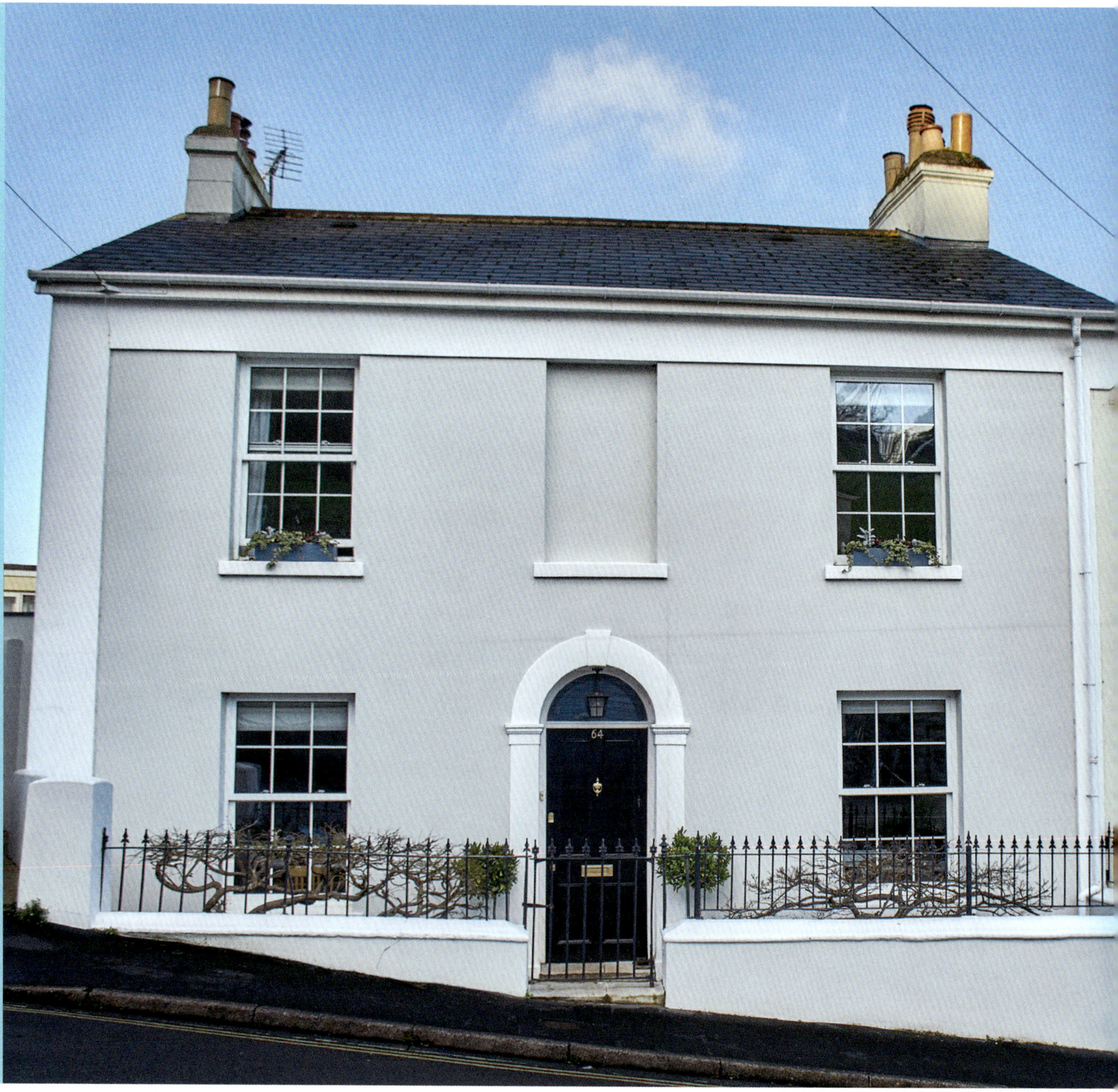

One of five handsome houses in St Leonard's Road

In a private road off St Leonard's Road is No 49, a substantial house at the foot of a large triangular field, sometimes called Aqua Villa. In the Market Hall is a poster advertising the business of the owner of this house – George Bibbings, master tripe dresser. He had a shop at No 59 East Street and was a respected tradesman. He was sworn in as a parish constable, and three years later in 1874 was elected to the powerful position of portreeve, effectively mayor, for the Reverend Richard Lane as Lord of the Manor of Wolborough. When George Bibbings's son married Mary Ruby Pascoe in 1876, his father had the local artillery fire cannon, the wedding party were drawn through the streets in carriages with matched grey horses and after the ceremony at the Salem Chapel, a vast wedding breakfast was served at the house. George Bibbings died at Aqua Villa in 1896, and three years later when his wife died the house was sold to William Paige, auctioneer. Upon his death, George Bibbings's daughter, Eliza Grace Bond bought back the family home.

At the top of St Leonard's Road, over 129 feet above sea-level, is Manor Crescent. The seven three-storey houses are noteworthy for the pierced woodwork of their bargeboards and porches. The seventh house was designed to blend in and yet is distinct with hood mouldings over the windows.

The stylish wooden bargeboards and porch canopies on a Manor Crescent house

Back Road

Off Wolborough Street is the ancient Back Road which still exists as access to Grafton Road and Berman Court, but peters out in a car park. Access by foot can still be made to cross the Union Bridge of 1822 over the River Lemon which now leads you to ASDA supermarket.

The Union Bridge is a grade II listed building protected since 1949, and built in Devon limestone. The adjoining walls were raised in 1982 as part of a flood prevention scheme by South West Water which added non-return flaps to the drainage pipes and a retaining dam at Holbeam.

The inscription reads 'The Union Bridge. Built by Subscription. 1822'.

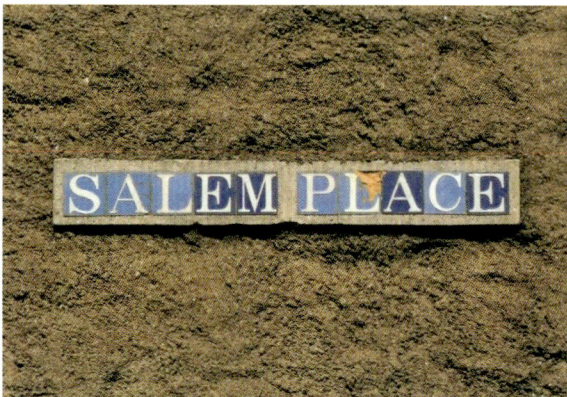

On Back Road, beside Salem Place, was once the Salem Chapel which held a memorial to Hannah Maria Bearne, benefactress of Bearne's School now in Queen Street. The chapel was demolished for road widening.

Wolborough Street once had many more houses and shops. Those that remain are blighted by the noise, dirt and proximity of traffic which must make it difficult to be house-proud. At some time it appears that any wide cornices over doors on the south side of the road have been removed or substantially narrowed to obviate collision by vehicles mounting the narrow pavement.

No 45 Wolborough Street is a grade II listed building, protected since 1972. It is a symmetrical late 1700s to early 1800s three-storey house sitting on a Devon limestone rubble plinth, with walls of painted Flemish bond brick (the brick is laid long side then short side). The eight sash windows are in moulded frames set forward in the wall under a flat brick splay. The ground- and first-floor windows are 8/8 panes, and the second floor has 4/8 panes. The six-panel door has a glazed top in a doorcase with panelled pilasters with fluted tops and a narrow cornice with small dentils. A boot scraper is inset in the wall.

No 45 Wolborough Street has had the added misfortune of having thirteen grilles punched through the front wall.

No 49, Wolborough Street, Tudor House, is a grade II listed building protected since 1983. It is a late 1500s two-storey house with a slate roof which was once thatched. The gable end faces the street like No 1 to 3 Wolborough Street as it is of a similar age. A shop front was inserted in the 1800s with an eight-pane window next to a modern door. Above is an off-centre casement window. The right hand wall in Pound Place has two massive chimney stacks. Between them is a modern door and casement windows, but most interesting is the tiny oblong window set between the floors. Pound Place was once where the stray cattle were impounded on market day. They were released to their owners on payment of a fee or toll. The pound keeper may have kept watch from this window. The old road surface revealed under the tarmac has limestone gulley stones and kerbs, granite setts and cobbles.

Pound Place's tiny window and lateral stack

Rooklands is a grade II listed building, protected since 1983. It is an early 1700s house now divided into three dwellings. The rear is approached through an ugly brick alleyway to Jubilee Road which was built in an orchard. This side of Rooklands shows the gable end with a coloured leaded window and decorative timberwork in a rendered cob and limestone rubble wall. There are three different windows on the rear wall and three tall cream brick chimney stacks in the steep slope of the once thatched roof.

Approached from Gothic Road, the front of Rooklands can be seen. There are two storeys with 1900s windows. Samuel Crooke lived cosily at 2, Rooklands in 1911 with his five children, wife, her three brothers and father, and a lodger.

No 55 Wolborough Street, the Wolborough Inn, is a grade II listed building, protected since 1983. It was converted from an early to mid-1800s three-storey house. The ground floor has two 1800s windows etched with the inn's name and old brewery on the plate-glass panes. The moulded cornices have incised key patterns to the pilasters. The four sash windows sit forward in the opening and are 8/8 panes on the first floor and 6/6 panes on the second floor. Ex-Navy man, Albert Ash, from Buckfastleigh, was innkeeper in 1911 before moving to the Half Moon Inn, now demolished, where he died in 1945.

No 63 Wolborough Street, Wolborough Manor House, is one of the oldest buildings in town, and is a grade II listed building, apparently protected since 1949. It was built in 1534 and is a three-storey house of thick cob walls under a slate roof with massive chimney stacks that are best seen over some charmless extensions, from Gothic Road.

A Regency stucco front was added. It now has nine 1900s casement windows. There is an elegant central porch with two Tuscan columns and two pilasters under a cornice and flat roof. The mid-1700s fluted and panelled door case is set back and has a wide six-panel door with a glazed top and a wrought-iron bell pull. There are red and black floor tiles surrounded by a tarmac car park which necessitated the demolition of part of the boundary wall and gateposts. The interior was subdivided in 1890 and after 1948 it has been offices for Truscott's toys, Manor Pottery, the British Legion and the Mid Devon Advertiser. The fine oak staircase has been removed, but thankfully it still has magnificent Jacobean plaster ceilings adorned with foliage, Tudor roses and the Opinicus, the heraldic beast of plasterers, with an eagle's head and wings, a lion's body and legs and a camel's tail.

The rear view of Wolborough Manor House shows the massive stacks and old windows.

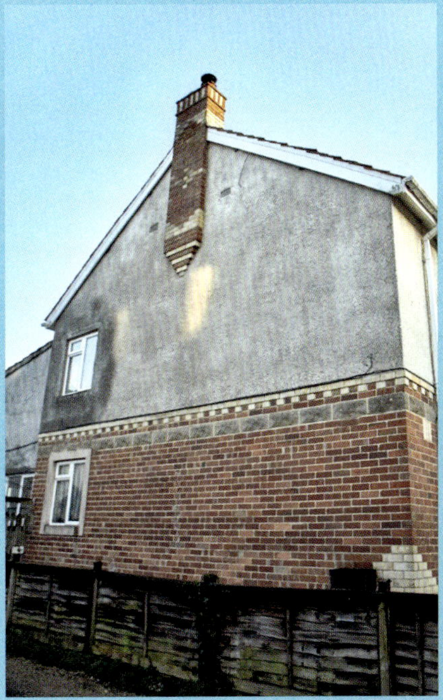

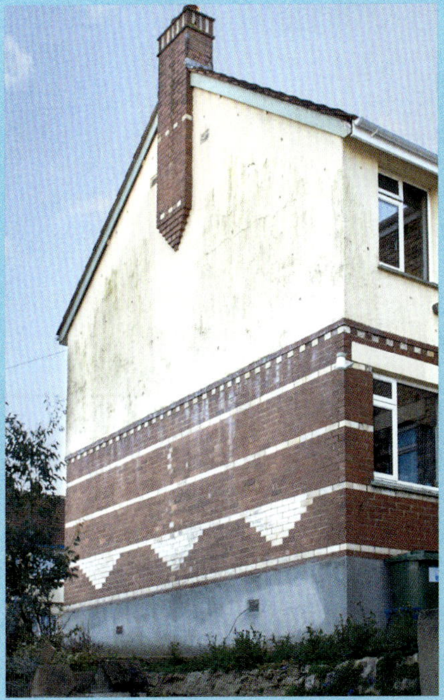

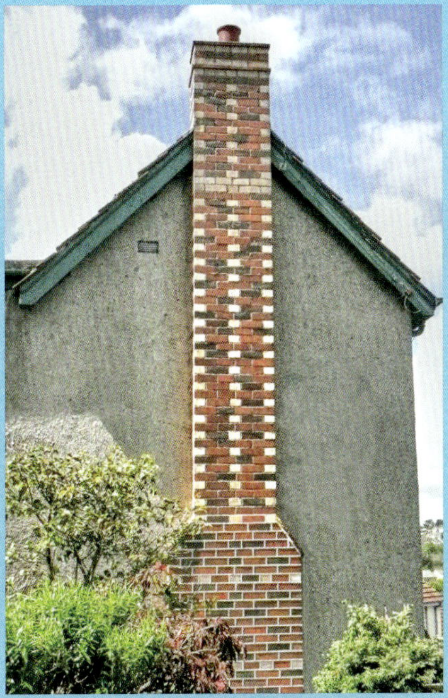

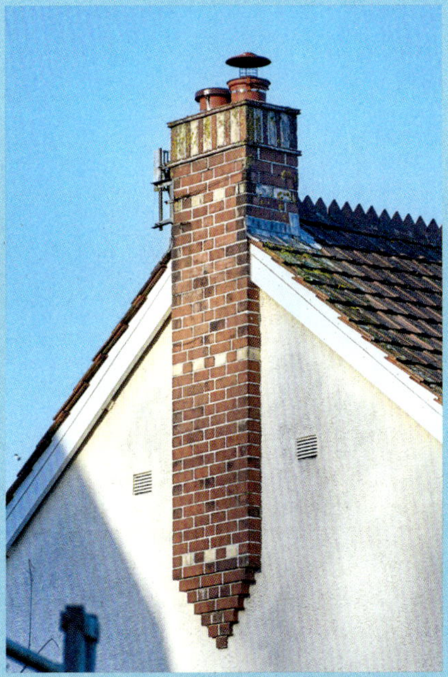

The complex brickwork of No 1 to 31 Jubilee Road

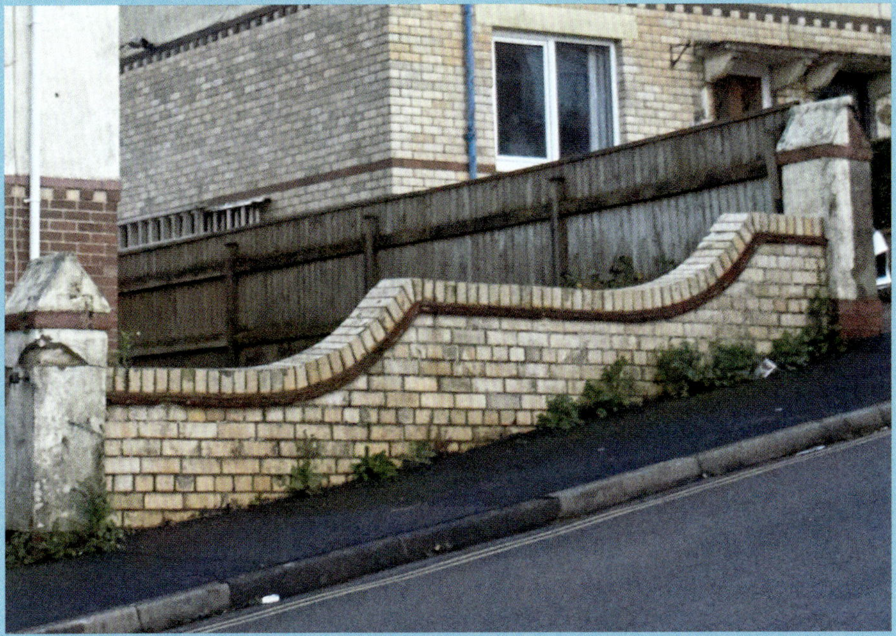

Jubilee Road

No 1 to 31 Jubilee Road have some of the nicest brickwork in town. The boundary walls swoop down the hill, and the detailing on the chimneys and walls are complex patterns in cream and red brick of ziggurats and diamonds, of plain and chequered horizontal or angled bands, capped with zig-zag ridge tiles on the roof – a delight in brick.

Left to right are No 65 and 67 Wolborough Street.

No 65 and 67 Wolborough Street are grade II listed buildings, protected since 1972. No 65 is a 1600s asymmetrical, two-storey house. The rounded uneven walls indicate it is made from cob which was mud mixed with straw and so should never be exposed to rainwater. The door is set back on the left-hand side. None of the four windows are the same and are a random mix of 6/6, 12/12 and 4/8 sash windows and a tri-part, four-pane casement. In 1911 Ellen Strudwick lived here with her four children whilst her husband was with his father working as a chauffeur to a doctor in Guildford.

No 67 is stepped back from No 65 and is an early 1800s two-storey house with an attic, which has added a new front to an earlier house. The painted stucco walls are not vertical and rise to a steeply pitched slate roof with a gabled dormer. The doorway has a narrow cornice supported by two simple consoles, as do No 69 and 70, which may indicate they all lost their wider cornices at the same time. The 1911 occupant was Henry Perryman, a porter in a coal yard – perhaps in Bearne's Lane.

No 69 and 71 Wolborough Street

No 69 and 71 Wolborough Street are grade II listed buildings, protected since 1972. They are a pair of mirror-image three-storey houses of the late 1700s to early 1800s with painted stucco walls. The doors are set at the outer edge of each house with a two-pane overlight under matching narrow cornices. Each house has an 8/8 sash window per floor. Joining the two houses is a band of modillions supporting the roof. No 69 had two families in 1911, William Sanders worked at John Vicary's Tannery, but Maria Langworthy had a private income.

No 73, Wolborough Street, Bushel House, is a grade II listed building, protected since 1972, and dates from the 1700s. It is set back from its neighbours with a forecourt of Devon limestone slabs. It is asymmetrical with limestone rubble walls which were formerly rendered and now reveal the signs of the remodelling of an earlier building. The door is set back on the right, although the vertical jointing of stone nearby indicates that it may have been wider. The ground floor has two 8/8 hornless sash windows with two more off-set above. There are three continuous timber lintels between the storeys which may have held a string course decoration and a change in rubble size above the second-storey windows indicates the front wall was raised in height to add the two attic rooms. In 1911 James Pitt lived here on his own. He described himself as an artist.

The double front doors have two different carved panels with angry birds and two green man masks.

No 75 and 77 Wolborough Street, Barchington House

No 73 Wolborough Street, Bushel House, may be named after the Bushel family of the neighbouring parish.

No 75 and 77 Wolborough Street, Barchington House, is a grade II listed building, protected since 1972. It is an early to mid-1800s two-storey symmetrical house with painted render walls. There are two 8/8 hornless sash windows on the ground-floor and three on the first-floor. The wide eaves have supporting brackets. It is now divided into two houses but in 1911 it was occupied by George Jordan, his wife, two sons and a lodger. George and his son were horsemen on a local farm, whereas the other son was a labourer in a brickyard – perhaps Decoy or Kingsteignton. The lodger was a tailor.

The doorway is a wide-arched recess with vermiculated voussoirs that look like worm casts in mud and a mascaron of a lady's head as the keystone at the top.

No 79 and 79a Wolborough Street

No 81 and 81a Wolborough Street

No 79 and 79a Wolborough Street is a grade II listed building, protected since 1972. It is a mid-1800s two-storey house now divided into two homes accessed through the right-hand panelled door under a heavy concrete lintel with no cornice. The rendered wall is incised to look like stone and each floor has two horned sash windows. In 1911 widower Garnett Willcocks was a nurseryman, probably at St Cuthberts Nursery along Wolborough Street and next door was Edwin Bowden, a mason.

No 81 and 81a Wolborough Street is a grade II listed building protected since 1972. It is a late 1700s to early 1800s two-storey house of rubble limestone remodelling an earlier building. Most of the render has been removed revealing the rough stone and cob work where the roof has been raised. There are three ground-floor 8/8 hornless sash windows and three first-floor 6/6 hornless sashes. The deep recess to the left may have been a court entrance, but now holds a door under a heavy concrete lintel with no cornice. A wide planked door in the wall to the right has a pintle for hanging a gate. The 1911 occupants were William Gollop and his son who were market gardeners, also at St Cuthbert's, and Thomas Hutchings an able seaman in the Royal Navy.

The porch frieze of No 83 Wolborough Street has triglyphs with guttae separated by patera.

No 83 Wolborough Street

No 83, Wolborough Street is a grade II listed building, protected since 1983. It is a symmetrical two-storey detached house built in the 1840s from ashlar Devon limestone on a large block plinth. Old maps indicate it was once occupied by John Lethbridge, famed for inventing the diving machine and who died here in 1759 – presumably in an earlier house. By 1911 it was occupied by Mary Northcott, widow of Richard who had farmed Hyner at Christow, and her single daughter. This is the only house in Wolborough Street that had a live-in servant.

The front of the building is in three parts. The outer two ranges have stone clasping pilasters which wrap around the corners of the house, with painted, moulded capitals at the top. The ground floor and first floor windows are hornless sashes except the central window which is a casement. All the windows are set in moulded architraves with two brackets under the sills.

The central range is stepped forwards and has a shallow porch like a small Greek temple. It has two shallow stone steps up to the doorway flanked by two free-standing fluted Doric columns and two pilasters attached to the wall behind. Above the columns is a frieze which has three vertical ridges called a triglyph separated by circular mouldings called patera. Below the triglyph are six little pegs called guttae. The door has six panels and the overlight above has nine small oval panes.

There is a flat-arched entrance on either side of the house and a paved forecourt spans front, protected by spearhead railings. Two boot scrapers hark back to a time of muddy streets.

The wall to the left has a curious metal rope-edged shield with the head of an otter holding a fish in its mouth. The letter A on the left has lost its companion.

No 85 and 87 Wolborough Street

No 89 Wolborough Street, Blanche House

No 85 and 87 Wolborough Street are grade II listed buildings, protected since 1983. They were built as one symmetrical house but it has been divided into an asymmetrical pair of houses. No 85 has stucco walls incised to look like stone, has removed the plat band which divided the storeys and has two 6/6 hornless sash windows in thin frames. No 87 has three of the same windows. There are two doorways in the centre, set back from the front of the house and without a sheltering cornice.

The matching doors have a zig-zag moulding to the lintel and a two-pane overlight. The roof has three small gabled dormers. Joseph Ingerson lived at No 85. He worked in a coal store, maybe with Mr Perryman at No 67. At No 87 was Ernest Hellens, a master builder. One son was his apprentice, but the other worked in the Home and Colonial shop. The larger house had a lodger. Florence Singleton was a bookkeeper for a grocers in 1911.

No 89 Wolborough Street, Blanche House, is a grade II listed building protected since 1972. It is an early 1800s symmetrical two-storey house with a plinth sitting below painted stucco walls. There are four 8/8, and one central 6/6 hornless sash windows. The central doorway has a narrow cornice sitting on rectangular brackets. There were three families here in 1911. George Drake was a plasterer, Louis Smith was a cab driver and Sarah Walling was a domestic cook, perhaps for Mary Northcott at No 83.

Pomeroy Road

Pomeroy Road has two matched rows of charming terraced cottages in crazy-paving limestone with red brick detailing around the windows and doors. The splay brick at the foot of the wall shows the rows step down to the River Lemon. The road may take its name from the nearby toll bar to the Totnes, Bridgetown Pomeroy Turnpike Trust road, but also may have been named after a 1900 action in the South African War under Devon's General Buller.

After Pomeroy Road, at a right-angle to the street and difficult to see, is No 92 Wolborough Street, now Kingsley House but once named West End Cottage as it historically marked the west end of the town of Newton Abbot. It is a grade II listed building protected since 1996. The two-storey house was built between 1840 and 1850 of stucco, incised to look like stone. There are three 6/6 unhorned sash windows on the first floor with closely spaced modillions under the eaves. There is a veranda with a glass roof supported by slender iron columns behind the high boundary wall.

Waltham Road

Waltham Road is a stylish group of cottages which starts with six houses flanking the entrance from Wolborough Street. Built in 1892 from crazy-paving local stone with dark red brick detailing around the windows and doors, they have a sill-level string course which shows the gradual descent to the River Lemon. The road has retained the local limestone kerbstones and an almost complete set of brick gateposts topped with stepped pyramids. One house has four unusual wall plates, and another has an original boot scraper by the front door.

Linden Terrace

The 15 houses of Linden Terrace were built in 1879/80 by William Brook Adams and his son, who both lived at No 13 for a while. The land was owned by the Earl of Devon and the houses designed by Joseph W. Rowell, his architect. The terrace started with a large house on Wolborough Street named Linden, lived in by James Snelling Bearne of the Bearne's Lane family.

In painted stucco, alternate houses have gables, a raised border band and string course with two arched windows on the first floor and an oriel window in the apex. The ground floor has a single window and a tall doorway with an overlight. Some of the houses retain their 4/4 sash windows, all retain their elegant chimney stacks. A footbridge at the end of the road leads over the River Lemon to Back Lane.

On the corner of Linden Terrace and Wolborough Street is a triangular granite block which has 'NB' inscribed on one side and 'TB' on the other. It is thought to mark the Newton Bar on the Totnes Bridgetown Pomeroy Turnpike Trust road. This turnpike was first created in 1759 as the local gentry of Newton Bushel and Newton Abbot complained that the road was 'ruinous, very incommodious and dangerous to travellers'. In 1823 the tolls taken at the Newton Bar totalled £106, rising to £353 in 1825. This money was used to fill potholes, empty gullies and build or repair bridges. Fines were imposed if you

The Newton Bar stone on the Totnes Bridgetown Pomeroy Trust turnpike road

Mr Rellend built this house at St Cuthbert's Nursery.

travelled the road but didn't pay the toll. The NB side of the stone has also been incised with the Ordnance Survey bench mark and maps indicate this point is 37 feet above sea level.

At one time there were two fields opposite Linden Terrace called Barn Field and Step Meadow, later occupied by St Cuthbert's Nursery. This was run by James Rellend from 1888 growing strawberries, grapes and peaches in a greenhouse over 160 feet long and had vegetable and flower beds in the field. He lived above the shop at 15/17 Courtenay Street where he sold his produce but

later built a distinctive red brick house on the nursery site. The nursery was sold for housing in 1926 but retained much of its original stone wall along Linden Terrace and Wolborough Street. No 15/17 Courtenay Street was demolished, and architect J. Archibald Lucas designed the Westminster Bank which replaced it in about 1928. The houses built on the St Cuthbert's site are mainly substantial semi-detached brick and render house, five of which were built for police officers. Some of the 1911 residents of Wolborough Street worked for Mr Rellend.

Mackrell's Almshouses and the boundary wall are at the end of Wolborough Street before it becomes Totnes Road, and is a grade II listed building protected since 1983. The building illustrates two architectural features which distinguish the work of Joseph W. Rowell — the use of Devonian limestone in a crazy-paving pattern and the shouldered or Caernarvon arch which can be seen on many of his designs around Newton Abbot and beyond.

The two continuous two-storey terraces are now divided into 38 flats and sit high above the road level. Joseph W. Rowell designed the almshouses in Gothic style and they were built by Hugh Mills for £5,000 in 1874/75 for Thomas Mackrell (1791–1883) one of the town's many benefactors. He had been born at No 5 Bank Street and as a child had played in the orchard here. After a career as a chemist in Barnstaple, and having inherited a considerable wealth from his family, he bought the orchard for £500 from the Earl of Devon and endowed £5,000 for running costs and for pensions

for the retired local trades people of good character housed here. The second terrace was designed by Joseph W. Rowell in 1894 for Sophia Mackrell (1804–1892), Thomas's sister. The overall impression of the terrace is one of repetitive units, but subtle differences deserve attention.

Thomas Mackrell's terrace starts with a house for the matron which sits forward from the rest of the units and has a four-bay window on the ground floor. Beyond this are six roof gables which are matched to five entrance gables leading onto the veranda and the front doors. Stepped forward from these units is a buttressed entrance which is topped by a weathervane. There is a simple inscription in the tympanum above this Caernarvon arch entrance. Following this is the second terrace of six roof gables and five entrance gables. A quatrefoil decoration holds the unit numbers for Thomas' twelve units.

Sophia Mackrell's terrace continues with an almost imperceptible change in angle (surprisingly best seen from the

The first terrace of Mackrell's Almshouse

first floor of the Passmore Edwards Centre) with a buttressed entrance which sits forward of the terrace and is topped by a metal finial. There is a longer inscription in the tympanum above this Caernarvon arch entrance. Following this are a terrace with six roof gables matched to six entrance gables. The last unit sits forward of the terrace and was a house for a chaplain.

Thomas's ground-floor windows have three lights under a shallow arch whereas Sophia's have four-light windows. All lower windows borrow light from a glass panel in the slate roof of the veranda. The use of Caernarvon arches and trefoil arches changes according to the unit.

The 180-metre long boundary wall to Mackrell's Almshouses is of Devon rubblestone crazy-paving with stepped and chamfered coping stones. There are four entrances flanked by gate piers and hung with wrought-iron gates. The gates leading to the two central entrances have carved trefoil caps and the other two have stepped pyramids. It is a complex building.

Living here in 1901 were 39 people who had retired from various trades, but included three nurses and a teacher. Most were dependent on both the roof the Mackrells provided and his pension, although three had some private money.

Steppes Meadow

Steppes Meadow (Teignbridge District Council's sign misspells the name) took its name from the original field name of Step Meadow. The semi-detatched houses which wrap around from Wolborough Street were built after 1926 when St Cuthbert's nursery was sold. They are red brick to the first-floor sill with shingle dash above. Each has a two-storey round bay and a semi-circular brick arch leading to a recessed entrance. There are some similar houses in Paynsford Road. The road ends at a footbridge over the River Lemon which leads to the Bradley Mills – a close association which caused problems of smoke, smells and noise when the Vicary Woollen Mills were working in 1957. Although they had been there since 1840, the site had doubled in size since 1939 and increased working hours to include a night shift, so burnt more coal. A successful appeal to the Rates Valuation Panel, reduced the rates for residents both here and in Linden Terrace.

Wolborough Church Path

Wolborough Church Path is the pedestrian route to the parish church of St Mary's, Wolborough. It has always been a steep path for the old, and muddy in the winter. Wolborough parishioners had a Chapel of Ease to enable them to attend services when the parish church was too difficult to get to – St Leonard's Chapel at the beginning of Wolborough Street.

Totnes Road

Totnes Road begins at the end of Wolborough Street and becomes the A381, but probably ends at Ogwell Cross.

On the right-hand side of Totnes Road is Bradley View, which has a blue plaque on the gatepost set in place by Newton Abbot Civic Society to commemorate it as the home of Oliver Heaviside.

In the right circles, Oliver Heaviside is known as a famous physicist, but to most ordinary people his work is impenetrable, yet many homes have the co-axial cable he invented leading to their televisions, satellite dishes and in the CCTV outside.

Oliver Heaviside was a 47-year-old bachelor when he moved to Bradley View in 1897. Few locals would have known that the eminent physicist and mathematician lived there, as he spent most of his time studying and theorising. He was deaf from scarlet fever, had bright red hair and piercing eyes which frightened children who regularly broke his windows, wrote unpleasant remarks on the front gate and trespassed from Baker's Park to steal from his fruit trees.

If only they had known – he had left school at 16 and had only one paid job as a telegraph operator, but by 1872, aged 22, he had published

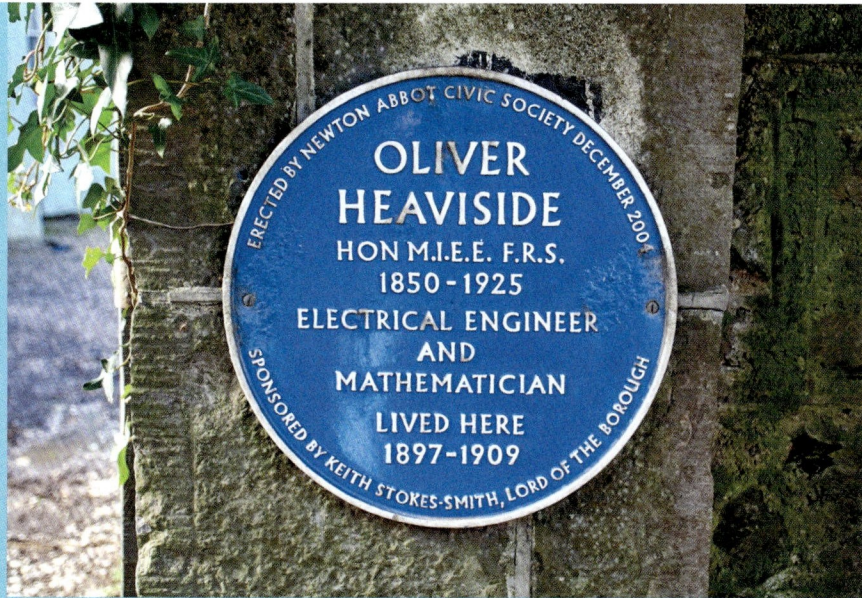

research on electric circuits and telegraphy and eight years later patented that coaxial cable. His work covered theories on electromagnetic induction to correct the distortion on telephone and telegraph lines, and on electromagnetic mass still discussed in astrophysics today.

In 1896 friends and admirers secured a civil-list pension for him of £120 per year and in 1897 he rented this house where he lived in near poverty so close to Mackrell's Almshouses. Yet it was here in 1902 that he proposed a theory to explain why Marconi's first radio signals sent across the Atlantic had curved around the Earth and not gone in a straight line out to space. Oliver predicted that the wireless waves were 'caught' by an ionised layer in the upper atmosphere and 'conducted' between this and the sea or land below. The existence of this layer was not proved until 1923/4, but it was called the Heaviside Layer. He frequently had to defend his theories, once saying 'I do not refuse my dinner simply because I do not understand the process of digestion.'

After a serious illness in 1908 he moved to Torquay where he grew increasingly isolated and eccentric until a fall in 1924 precipitated his death in February 1925.

_____

An advert for a 3½ litre Jaguar made in Coventry in 1947 showed the stately car posed in front of Bradley Manor which it described as a 'charming 15th century house, property of the National Trust'. Although it is not known if the Jaguar still exists, and nothing is known about the Jaguar's owner, plenty is known about the owners of Bradley Manor and when you visit and buy the booklet, it will tell you the manor house is 13th century not 15th!

The written history of the Manor of Highweek and Bradley Manor house starts with a butler and passes through kings to nobles to the Bushel family from 1262 to 1405, the Yardes until 1751, the Veale family and their heir Reverend Richard Lane until 1842, the Reverend Frederick Wall then his daughter until 1903, the Scratton trustees until 1909. It was then bought by Cecil Firth of Ashburton, an Egyptologist and a distant relative of the Yarde family, who left it to his daughter, Diana Woolner, who gave it to the National Trust in 1938. At many stages of wealth and decline, refurbishment and restoration, the building has been added to and subtracted from, and an absorbing model in the house allows you to follow these through the ages.

This book has noticed only part of the history of Newton Abbot's buildings and the people and events that they have seen. Of any building mentioned there is more depth to its history, of each person mentioned there is more of their life to be discovered, of any event referred to there are more reasons behind it. It is intended to write a second book to cover other roads in Newton Abbot not mentioned here, including the story of this building, Forde House.